34LR

ADVENTURE PLAY
WITH HANDICAPPED CHILDREN

By the same author

DISABLED WE STAND

HUMAN HORIZONS SERIES

ADVENTURE PLAY WITH HANDICAPPED CHILDREN

ALLAN T. SUTHERLAND and PAUL SOAMES

A CONDOR BOOK
SOUVENIR PRESS (E & A) LTD

362.78

Contents

Acknowledgements

The quotations from Lady Allen of Hurtwood on pages 16–17 and 38 are taken from the Handicapped Adventure Playground Association's booklet, *Adventure Playgrounds for Handicapped Children*; we wish to thank HAPA for giving us permission to use them. We also wish to thank Dr Charles Pocock for allowing us to print the observations quoted on page 27 and page 50, which are taken from a personal communication to one of the authors.

We are very grateful to Pat Fairon and the Children's Scrap Project, London, for permission to use the material quoted on pages 95–99, which is taken from an article in the July 1983 issue of *Play Times*.

We are particularly indebted to the four photographers who, having already donated their time and professional skills to HAPA, willingly gave us permission to reprint the photographs which appear in the centre section of this book: Bob Bray, Camilla Jessel, Tilly Odell and Patrick Sutherland.

Introduction

Play is a highly serious business. It is not merely a method of passing the time, but a child's most important method of learning, through which he or she develops physical and mental skills, gains self-confidence and independence and learns to interact socially with other people. A child who is deprived of adequate opportunities for play is being denied the chance to develop these physical, emotional and imaginative capabilities to the full.

This is true of all children, but it is especially important in the case of children with disabilities, who are particularly likely to be denied chances for play. Children with limited mobility are restricted by inadequate access; many mentally handicapped children remain stuck indoors because they can not safely be allowed out on their own; many other children simply need a chance to develop a bit of self-confidence, or to take things at their own pace. Most existing play provision caters only for able-bodied children, with little or no attention to the particular needs of children with disabilities. In particular, they tend to be deprived of opportunities to play in ways that are active, adventurous and exciting, that present them with challenges and help them to meet those challenges. This deprivation does enormous harm; we know that to be true because we have seen, again and again, astonishing changes taking place in those children who use the playgrounds on which we have worked, which exist to provide such opportunities.

We have written this book to be both a campaigning document and a practical manual, to explain how important it is that children with disabilities should be given the chance to play adventurously and to provide detailed information for people who want to give them that chance, or who are already involved in doing so. We hope that it will be read by, among others, parents and teachers of children with disabilities, the workers and management of existing handicapped adventure playgrounds, people who are currently trying to set up an adventure playground for handicapped children or are interested in doing so, those who have a more general interest in adventure play as a method of provision of play facilities for all children and anybody else who is concerned about the welfare of children with disabilities.

Because this book is, in part, a practical manual for people who are working to provide the kind of play facilities that we describe, we have written a number of chapters, such as those on resources and equipment, in such a way that they can be treated as independent, relatively self-contained guides to the subject in question. This has, inevitably, meant that there is a certain amount of overlap between chapters. We would also point out that much of the information and advice we include in these chapters could equally well be applied to ordinary adventure playgrounds or, more generally, to other types of community-based projects, such as youth clubs or playgroups.

Obviously, there are limits to the amount of information that can be presented in a book of this size. We have tried, however, when we feel that more detailed information may be required than we have room to give, to guide our readers to where that information may be found. We would recommend therefore, particularly those readers who are using this book as a guide to setting up a playground or other project, that they use the reference section at the end of the book in conjunction with the text.

In preparing this book, we have consulted a great many people in the play movement, all of whom have willingly given us the benefit of their experience. We hope they will forgive us if we do not list them all individually, but simply express our gratitude to them all: this would have been a lesser book without their help.

1 The Need for Handicapped Adventure Play

Play is crucial to the development of all children, whether disabled or not. Lloyd George summed up its importance seventy years ago as follows:

> The right to play is the child's first claim on the community. Play is nature's training for life. No community can infringe that right without doing deep and enduring harm to the bodies and minds of its citizens.

Through play children learn to grow and develop emotionally, intellectually and physically. Mobility, co-ordination, perception, balance, sharing, relating, awareness of space, colour, sound, touch and other people – all of these and more are integral parts of the play process. Without those experiences children become emotionally stunted and intellectually deprived, and less able to face the world adequately as they grow and mature into adulthood.

So what is so special about adventure play, particularly in relation to disability? In our opinion an adventure playground can provide one of the most satisfactory play opportunities for any child: large outdoor spaces, often of an acre or more, with climbing frames, slides, swings, water and sand play, barbecues and areas for ball games, animals, bikes and go-karts; indoor space where craft work, cooking, reading and games, ranging from board games to dressing-up activities, can take place. But the single most important distinguishing feature of an adventure playground is the presence of one or more full-time staff who offer support and guidance to the children, as well as maintaining and developing the site.

They are places where activities ranging from the structured and organised to the unstructured and spontaneous can happen, and, crucially, an environment and atmosphere where the children themselves feel they have control and a say in what goes on.

Three words sum up what an adventure playground can offer: exploration, experimentation and expansion. These are particularly relevant concepts when looking at disabled children in adventure playgrounds, and the opportunity to carry out all three activities is central to the playground experience. Height, space, movement, mobility, touch and relationships all need to be explored and developed as confidence and familiarity grow. Experimentation with textures, colours, equipment and one's own ideas and limits lead to a greater understanding of the world around the individual as well as the individual's role within that world. If playgrounds can be built and developed around these challenging concepts then the potential benefits for children using them can be enormous.

One of the special features of an adventure playground should be its flexibility. For example, new play structures or swings can be built and dismantled at frequent intervals, and can also be constructed in such a way that additions and adaptations can be carried out with relative ease. Similarly, if children want to build their own camps there should be enough space and materials on site for them to do this. Ultimately, an adventure playground should be able to provide such a range of opportunities that all children who visit the project can be both occupied and satisfied, even if that activity consists of sitting quietly in a corner reflecting or reading a book.

If we believe that it is important to give children the mental and physical space to grow and develop, the need for such projects, along with other forms of play provision, in our increasingly competitive and child-alienating world, is enormous. This need is most apparent in our towns and cities, where busy roads, polluted environments and dense, ill-designed housing areas restrict play opportunities, but it is also important that such opportunities should exist in more rural regions. Restricted access to land used by farmers, the armed services and landowners, dangerous agricultural machinery, the use of pesticides, spaces within small towns and villages which are reserved for sports activities or as show for tourists, dangerous country roads – any of these can militate against the provision of play space and so deprive children of play experiences. It is important to remember, therefore, that we are talking about the play needs of all children, wherever they may live. Indeed, almost half of the existing adventure playgrounds for handicapped children are situated in more rural country areas.

If we accept that play is of paramount importance to children's development, then the need for adventure play opportunities for children with disabilities quickly becomes apparent when we start to look at their disabled experience: enclosed indoor environments; a life bounded much of the time by the four walls of school, hospital, home, hostel or training centre. A life often bounded, too, by structure and organisation, invariably arranged by other people, means that the chance to play is often severely limited, if not almost non-existent for many of these people; this applies both to mentally and to physically handicapped people.

The sheer physical and emotional frustration these restrictions can impose on disabled children is often vividly illustrated, when a visit to an adventure playground is made, by the explosion of energy and activity that takes place. Indeed, it can take some time for children who have had limited play experience to 'settle down' into a playground, and space has to be given for them to adapt and get used to a large outdoor area which has few obvious restraints.

Many of the environments familiar to children with disabilities are those where noise, untidiness and freedom of movement and expression are limited. An adventure playground offers a change, and the maximum opportunity for users to give vent to their thoughts, feelings and ideas.

It is, of course, not our contention that school, hospital, home and other forms of provision operate a continually sterile, unstimulating environment; they have their own particular, valid function to perform, which playgrounds must be aware of, and co-operate with. What we do feel, however, is that too often the play needs of disabled children are not adequately met in these facilities, or are met by token efforts. If such children have access to an adventure playground, along with other types of play provision, such as a toy library, this lack of experience can be rectified.

The benefits to be gained from adventure play are by no means nebulous: it brings about changes that are concrete, observable and in some cases dramatic – particularly so in the case of children with disabilities. A couple of examples should make this clear.

David has Down's Syndrome. At the time of this story he was in his late teenage years. In the middle of the night the house in which he lived with his family caught fire. David's bedroom was situated at the top of the house. He could not be reached internally once the fire had taken hold. By the time the fire brigade arrived everybody in the house, except David, was safely outside.

The family were very frightened for David's safety, because they thought that he was afraid of heights and was not mobile enough to use a ladder. To their astonishment, as soon as the fireman's ladder was erected and placed by his window David calmly clambered out, and down, without any fuss at all. It is the firm belief of his parents that, but for his experience of climbing steps and ladders and experiencing the heights of play structures at the adventure playground he used, and the confidence this had given him, he might not have survived the fire.

John was ten years old. He had had a very serious accident which had necessitated a year's hospitalisation. When he came out, he was educationally backward through having missed a year's schooling, emotionally immature as a result of his long period in hospital and lack of contact with other people during that time, and physically weak and unco-ordinated.

He was placed on an adventure playground for three months full-time, and then spent part of his time back at school and part on the playground until he was completely integrated back into his former school. From coming on to the project as an extremely delicate and frightened child, he gradually grew and developed, physically and mentally, into a robust, articulate boy. His co-ordination and communication skills improved dramatically. More of a struggle was his association with other children of his own age, but this too developed as time went by.

Of course there were other people involved in John's rehabilitation, notably his parents and school, but all agree that his experience of attending an adventure playground hastened his recovery and improved his physical and mental condition beyond anybody's initial expectations.

These are two dramatic examples. Similar ones can be found, but the vast majority are probably of a more limited nature, though no less important for the individuals involved: small improvements in co-ordination and balance gained from riding bikes or climbing structures; improved communication skills from mixing with other children and sharing activities; finer appreciation of textures and colours from experimenting with sand, water and paints; an awareness of danger and excitement from cooking on open fires or flying high on swings. All these experiences can be had in an adventure playground and offer the chance for development and progress to the people concerned.

For further evidence of the positive work that is engaged in on handicapped adventure playgrounds we would refer readers to two studies carried out on one project during the 1970s: *The Adventure Playground as a Therapeutic Environment* (1980), by Paul Wolff, a professor from California Polytechnic State University, and Sophie Levitt's *A study of the gross motor skills of cerebral palsied children in an adventure playground for handicapped children*. Further details of these studies are given in the reference section at the back of this book.

The restricted environments and experiences that many disabled children and adults come from or know place pressures upon them – pressures ranging from having to live highly organised lives to relying on other people for such basic facilities as transport. An adventure playground, however temporarily, can relieve that pressure; indeed it should be designed to do so. Of course there are important areas to be aware of, such as toileting and drug needs, but these must not cloud the purpose of the children's attendance at an adventure playground, a purpose which revolves around the concepts of fun, enjoyment and personal fulfilment in a free and permissive atmosphere.

We should perhaps point out at this stage that there have been, and still are, some sceptics about the worth of adventure playgrounds for handicapped children. We would argue that most of these people either have a limited understanding of what such projects are about and what philosophy lies behind them, or have themselves had a negative experience of an adventure playground. (Even we would admit that there are *some* bad schemes!)

Overwhelmingly, though, the response of lay and professional people who have seen a good adventure playground in action is a positive one. Indeed, many people have seen aspects of children that they never thought existed, or had only glimpsed briefly at home or in the classroom. One of the authors can remember the amazement of a parent when she saw her child riding a bicycle independently for the first time – she had thought that the child would never be able to manage such a feat. The experience brought tremendous satisfaction to both parent and child.

A playground can expose and develop new sides of children with disabilities, and help concerned adults to become aware of these and work to extend them. Indeed, playgrounds have the potential to help children break through into a new and exciting world.

It is appropriate to finish this chapter with a quotation from Lady Allen of Hurtwood who was the inspiration behind the birth of the adventure playground movement in this country, a quotation which introduces an idea that we shall explore in greater depth in the rest of this book:

All children need a place to play. They need space, informality, freedom to run around and make a noise, to express themselves, to experiment and investigate. Mentally and physically handicapped children and young people need this freedom even more than others. In surroundings which stimulate their imagination and challenge them to face and overcome risks, they will be helped to build up their self-confidence and independence . . . We hope that what began as one local pioneering experiment will grow into a national effort and that adventure playgrounds for the handicapped will become a recognised way of helping disabled young people take their place in the wider community.

2 How it all Started

The beginnings of the concept of adventure play were formulated in the early 1930s by the Danish landscape architect C. Th. Sørensen. Sørensen had designed a number of playgrounds, but noticed that children preferred to play in places like junk yards and building sites, where they could invent their own activities with the materials that were lying around. Where many adults would have simply dismissed such activities, Sørensen realised that there were good reasons for their choice: these places gave children opportunities that were not present in the playgrounds that were being purpose-built for them: opportunities to build, to dig holes, to experiment, to exercise their imaginations and to get on with the serious business of play with a minimum of adult intervention.

Sørensen's major insight was to realise that what was wrong with purpose-built playgrounds was precisely the fact that they were purpose-built: children need to be creators, not merely passive consumers, and the children Sørensen had noticed had been seeking out places where they could find a range of materials that they could turn to their own ends. He therefore suggested that, by providing children with a variety of waste materials and letting them get on with it, it would be possible to create 'a sort of junk playground in which children could create and shape, dream and imagine and make dreams and imagination a reality'.

These ideas were first put into practice over a decade later, when Emdrup playground was established in 1943, during the German occupation of Denmark. It was set up at the centre of a large new housing development on the outskirts of Copenhagen, and had the great advantage of being planned as an integral part of that development rather than as a later addition. It was surrounded by a six-foot-high bank, on top of which was a fence shielded by plants, an arrangement which both created a feeling of privacy for the children using the playground and ensured that it would not be troubled by complaints about noise or messiness from the occupants of the surrounding flats. From the very beginning, therefore, it provided an environment which belonged to the children rather than to adults – an essential feature of adventure playgrounds as we have come to know them.

That freedom was further ensured by the approach to his work of Emdrup's first leader, John Bertelsen, a former seaman and trained nursery school teacher. Bertelsen believed strongly that his role on the playground was as a facilitator, not an organiser: the initiative must remain with the children. He also, as Joe Benjamin has pointed out, 'saw the playground as a place where children would have opportunities for constructive play *bearing upon the activities of the outside world*; where they "can play and spontaneously learn by playing" ', and appreciated how important it was that this should be a junk playground in more than just name – a place where children could get away from their well-ordered everyday existence and make their own decisions about their activities in a way that was not conditioned by adult preconceptions about what might be best for them.

Emdrup was an immediate success: the intense activity of the many children who flocked to use it demonstrated amply that Sørensen's suppositions about the nature of play were entirely justified. It gained considerable local support, partly perhaps because residents of the area could recognise the positive effect it was having on their children in the difficult social conditions of the German occupation. And it set an example to the rest of the world – an example which has been most strongly followed in Britain.

In March 1946 Emdrup was visited by Lady Allen of Hurtwood. Marjory Allen, a landscape architect and chair of the Nursery Schools Association, was an individual as re-markable as Sørensen or Bertelsen. She was both someone who cared passionately about what happened to children and a seasoned campaigner who believed in getting – and usually did get – results. (Her 1944 pamphlet, *Whose Children?*, dealing with conditions in residential children's homes, had caused a storm of controversy that led to the setting up of a Parliamentary Committee of Enquiry, and was to be an important influence on the 1948 Children Act.) She was greatly impressed by what she saw at Emdrup, as she later commented in her autobiography: 'In a flash of understanding I realised that I was looking at something quite new and full of possibilities.' On her return to England she started to publicise the idea, and wrote a major article for *Picture Post*, in which she described Emdrup as 'a democratic community in which the leader never organises groups or play, and where the children's freedom is limited only by their feeling of responsibility, by the atmosphere of the place, and by the care they take of other children . . .'

The article provoked great interest: as the response to *Whose Children?* had demonstrated, there was already considerable concern about the effect on children of the upheavals of the war and its aftermath. The extensive areas of bomb damage provided a considerable choice of possible playground sites, a fact recognised in the article's title: 'Why not use our bombed sites like this?' The existence of such sites also gave children an opportunity to demonstrate, in the clearest possible way, their preference for playing in places which offered more extensive opportunities than conventional playgrounds.

Britain's first junk playground was established in Camberwell, South London, in 1948, with the support of the Cambridge House Settlement, and ran for three years. Other projects followed, particularly as the National Playing Fields Association became increasingly committed to encouraging the growth of what were coming to be known as 'adventure playgrounds' – a term which was originally chosen simply to give 'junk' playgrounds a more positive public image, but was to come to mark an extension of Sørensen's original philosophy. Lady Allen joined the NPFA's Playground Committee in 1953, and continued to campaign for adventure play, emphasising in particular the importance of a continuous supply of movable materials and the central role of a good playleader. Her campaigning charisma and committee skills were amply complemented by the day-to-day energy and vision of W. D. Abernethy, the Secretary of the committee, whose activities and writings for the NPFA have played a significant role in the refining of Sørensen's original concept into the ideas of 'adventure play' as we now know it. The influence of these two figures was to lead the NPFA into becoming a major force in the development of adventure play in Britain.

These earliest playgrounds tended to be run on very limited resources, with a single underpaid and overworked playleader, often on sites that would later be reclaimed for development. Typically, although there were some notable exceptions, they ran for a few years before closing through loss of the site, lack of funds or lack of local support. (A number of these pioneer projects, and the lessons to be learnt from their experience, have been documented by Joe Benjamin in *Grounds for Play*.) They also tended, in the earliest days, to be working in isolation, with little opportunity to learn from the experience of projects that preceded them.

Lessons *were* learnt, nevertheless, and a body of experience began to grow, nourished by individual playworkers carrying their expertise from one project to another; by the growth of the NPFA's Play section and the establishment of other supporting organisations such as the London Adventure Playground Association (LAPA), the International Play Association and various regional play associations; and, eventually, by the growing number of playgrounds that were being set up on permanent sites, with adequate funding, which was increasingly being provided by local authorities who had come to recognise the value of such facilities. From the mid-1960s a major expansion started to take place: when Lady Allen became chair of the newly-formed LAPA in 1962, there were four adventure playgrounds in London; twelve years later, there were sixty-one, set up by a variety of statutory and voluntary bodies.

As the adventure playground movement has grown, there has been a corresponding development in ideas about what they should consist of. It is now widely recognised that an adventure playground should be a permanent facility, open all the year round, and that it should have strong links with its local community. The essential importance of high-quality, experienced playworkers is still recognised, but staffing levels are generally considerably higher: though some playgrounds are still restricted by lack of finance, it is recognised that it is desirable to have a minimum of three or four full-time workers, with additional support provided by volunteers and temporary workers employed during school holidays.

Where the earliest projects were largely geared to outdoor activities, most playgrounds now have permanent buildings, and make considerable use of them, recognising that free creativity can be an indoor as well as an outdoor activity. As well as the activities of building, digging, lighting fires and using movable materials that have formed the basis of adventure play from the very beginning, most playgrounds now attach a lot of importance to building play structures which create opportunities for climbing, swinging and sliding. Playgrounds have also become increasingly aware of the importance of health and safety criteria, particularly in relation to structure-building; this has partly been forced on playgrounds by legal requirements, but they have also come to recognise that adventure playgrounds can provide opportunities that are exciting and challenging without being dangerous, and that it is part of the responsibility of playground staff and management to maintain this balance.

But, although the philosophy of adventure play has developed over the forty years since Emdrup was set up, and although the adventure play movement continues to expand, the need for adventure play has increased vastly more. As the nature of our cities, and of urban life, has changed, children have become more and more restricted, further and further isolated from each other, from the adult world and from many of the opportunities that could be taken for granted as little as twenty years ago. Even with able-bodied children, therefore, we should remember that when an adventure playground is opened it is merely giving back to children a little of what has been taken away from them.

During her time with LAPA, Lady Allen became aware that these existing adventure playgrounds were not meeting the needs of one important group of children: children with disabilities. Her initial response was to start working with the Cheyne Centre for Spastic Children in Chelsea to set up a number of holiday clubs, which were initially started to cater for children with cerebral palsy, but rapidly expanded their membership to include children with a much wider range of disabilities. From the success of these clubs grew the idea of an adventure playground that would be open all year round, an idea backed by Sophie Levitt, the Centre's physiotherapist, who 'felt the children needed a place where they could learn, through free and adventurous play, how to meet the challenges denied them in a clinical environment and so prepare themselves for living in a wider community'. A small research committee, the Handicapped Adventure Playground Association, was formed, and in February 1970 the Chelsea Playground for Handicapped Children opened.

This venture had several similarities to Emdrup: it was an experimental project, but one that was based on a clearly-seen need, carefully planned in advance and adequately resourced. Like Emdrup, it set an example that was to be followed all over the world: the approach that was pioneered at Chelsea has served as a model for every adventure playground for handicapped children that has been established since then – some two dozen in fourteen years.

The playground catered for children with every sort of disability – physical, mental, sensory and emotional. It had two full-time members of staff and a purpose-built, fully wheelchair-accessible building. What has most strongly influenced other such playgrounds, however, has been the range of activities that were available to children using the playground, both indoors and outdoors: sand and water play, play structures presenting opportunities for climbing and a range of different swings and slides, making fires, and indoor activities such as woodwork, arts and crafts and cooking. Not all of these had been planned in advance; it had not been foreseen, for example, how popular cooking would be with the children, and subsequent playgrounds have tended to include much larger kitchens than the small space set aside for making cups of tea in the original Chelsea building.

As the playground developed, it was realised that the idea of an adventure playground as a place for children to play freely, with playworkers simply responding to their initiatives, was not entirely applicable to an adventure playground for handicapped children: many children with disabilities lacked the mobility, the confidence, or even the experience of how to play, just to be left to get on with it by themselves. The most important feature of Chelsea's approach to have been taken up by the handicapped adventure playground movement as a whole is the idea that such a playground must offer a range of activities that extends from the structured – such as craft or cooking sessions led by a playworker or adult volunteer – to the free play of the traditional adventure playground, where children structure their activities for themselves with a minimum of adult intervention.

The Chelsea playground was an extraordinary, and immediate, success. The numbers of children using it, and the distances from which they travelled, made it very clear that the need for such facilities in London was too great to be served by a single playground. HAPA opened three more playgrounds in the mid-1970s, in Fulham, Islington and Wandsworth, and were later to open a fifth, the Charlie Chaplin playground in Kennington, Lambeth. The original Chelsea playground closed in 1982, as its site was being sold by the owners, the Church of England, but at the time of writing it is about to re-open on a new site. The storm of protest that greeted the threat of closure demonstrated amply how important a part of its local community and the play world the project had become. But the strongest sign of the success of the original experiment can be found on two dozen sites all over Britain and scattered as far away as Israel, Australia and Japan, where children with disabilities are discovering self-confidence and independence on adventure playgrounds inspired by Chelsea's example.

3 Starting from Scratch

This chapter aims to offer practical advice to people who are interested in starting up an adventure playground for handicapped children. The assumption we are making is that several people have developed an interest in creating such a project and want to know what to do next. Much of the information contained here could equally well be used for starting up holiday or weekend playschemes.

Although the reference section of this book is relevant throughout, we do feel that it is of particular importance to this chapter. We therefore urge people who want to start a project to use the reference section and get hold of some of the material suggested.

Research
For people who want to set up the kind of play project discussed in this book, the first basic task is to carry out research into the feasibility of creating such a scheme.

Start by visiting several existing playgrounds, ideally those that are in areas similar to the place where you want to build yours. This will give you a good indication of the kind of issues you will be faced with in developing your project. Equally important is the visual image that will remain with you, and help you formulate your aims and objectives for the scheme. Most existing playgrounds do welcome visitors and are only too pleased to talk about the pitfalls and problems they have encountered, and the strategies they have adopted.

It is useful to make notes on such visits, covering subjects from types of play structures seen to PR and fund-raising methods used. These notes can be taken back and used in your discussions and will help in planning.

Do not, however, try to carbon-copy what appears to be a good existing playground. It has been known for people to imitate other projects to the extent of trying to plan almost identical buildings, pathways, structures and landscapes. Fortunately, none of these proposed projects has materialised. Each playground is, and should be, unique in its development and style. Learn from others but retain your own originality and ideas.

Once you have seen several other projects and gained a general picture of what you are aiming for, start to research locally.

First and most obviously, is there a need? Is there an existing adventure playground nearby or do any playschemes operate? In an inner city area there may be a project a few miles away, but is it able to cater for as many children as might want to use it? In the Greater London area, for instance, there are eight handicapped adventure playgrounds which are by no means reaching all the children that could use them. There is therefore a need for more.

Explore the need at this early stage with people involved in the field of disability, such as special schools, the local MENCAP organisation, self-help parent groups, residential homes for disabled children, as well as individual parents and other professional workers. These are the people who will use the playground, so they must be consulted about how and when they could utilise it. Talking to these people will also give you a clear picture of the range of children for whom a project needs to cater. Then approach existing play projects and organisations such as playschemes, play groups, toy libraries and playbuses to see what they have to say.

This can be time-consuming, and you will not reach everyone – indeed, you might meet opposition on your round! – but it is crucial that you do this 'sounding-out' process, because you will not be able to develop such a project in isolation from everybody else.

You might at this stage come across an existing playscheme for children with disabilities that operates during the holidays or at weekends, in which case it might be useful to discuss with them the idea of working together to create a full-time adventure play project. The first handicapped adventure playground in Chelsea started from a holiday club for physically handicapped children. The advantage of this, of course, is that there would be some people and resources immediately available, and the task of getting an enthusiastic core group of people together would be already begun.

The object of this initial research is to get a more realistic picture of what you will need to do – how great a commitment is called for? what time-scale is involved? – a picture which will probably turn out to be different from the one with which you originally started out. Above all, this process will help you to firm up the aims and objectives which you will need to carry with you throughout the process of setting up the scheme. Dr Charles Pocock, Chairperson of the Basildon and District Adventure Playground for Handicapped Children, sums up the position succinctly by saying, 'Objectives need to be clearly established and all those involved should be single-minded in striving to achieve agreed objectives.'

Management

The initial sounding-out process should have thrown up several people who are interested in serving on a management committee; indeed, one of the aims of early research into the need should be to find people willing to serve on such a body.

It will take a number of meetings to get a strong enough group together, and it is worth taking time to do this. This group should ideally comprise a fairly wide range of people: parents, teachers, social service personnel, local authority officers or elected officials, health service staff, local representatives from relevant charitable bodies such as PHAB and MENCAP, people who are interested in fund-raising such as a representative from a local Lions or Rotary Club, plus interested lay people who live locally. We would recommend a group of 12–14 people as a good sized committee, bearing in mind that not everybody will be able to attend all the meetings.

At first the group will not be formally constituted, simply because it will not have had time to register as a charitable organisation. (We are talking here of voluntary projects, as opposed to those that are statutory-run.) This does not mean that it cannot do any work, or elect people to chair meetings and take minutes. One of its first tasks, however, when a large enough group has been assembled, will be to seek charitable status by applying to the Charity Commissioners (whose address can be found in the reference section) for registration as an independent charity. This involves drawing up a constitution, which the Commissioners need to approve. It is always useful to get hold of a copy of another project's constitution and use that as a basis from which to draw up your own. Also get the advice of a solicitor (a good person to get on the committee), who will help guide you through the whole process. It will take several months to do this – so be patient! While this is going on the committee can start work.

The first few gatherings should be spent on defining the previously mentioned aims and objectives – what are you aiming for? Once these have been established, you have to do the work of planning the most relevant and realistic course of action to get the project working. The first step here is to appoint a chairperson, vice-chairperson, secretary and treasurer to the group. These people will form the administrative base from which to operate the creation of the scheme. All four will need to be prepared to put a great deal of time and effort into the creation of the project. They will need easy access to telephones and typing and duplicating facilities, as well as some skills in negotiating and conducting meetings. Bear in mind that your committee does not have to be run solely by 'committee types': you should think about using positions such as vice-chairperson to let somebody who might lack confidence gain experience of committee work.

A *chairperson* is appointed to control a meeting, see that all the business is covered to everybody's satisfaction within a reasonable time, sum up arguments and debates, and bring discussions to a focus. They are also often the people who are asked to speak at public meetings or represent the body at other functions. It is an important post, particularly in the early stages of operating a playground, where they could be responsible for maintaining the enthusiasm and momentum of the people involved or interested in the project.

The *vice-chairperson* has to deputise for the chair and so must be equally aware of the above points. This is however a position with few formally defined responsibilities. It can be dispensed with. Or it can be used: to groom a future chairperson, or to give officer status to someone of obvious competence, providing an extra voice on those occasions when officers have to make a rapid decision on some matter that is too urgent to wait until the next full meeting.

The *secretary* is there to deal with the fundamental administration of the group: take and circulate minutes, arrange meetings and venues, deal with correspondence both to and from the committee, and generally service the whole scheme. There must be good communication between the chairperson and secretary, as in many ways they are the two pivotal people. It is our experience that where this relationship has broken down, either in the early stages of a project or when it is operating, great damage has been threatened and in some cases done. These two people will also be the ones to negotiate with outside bodies for funds, sites, resources and the like, making it even more imperative that they work closely together.

The position of *treasurer* is also important. He or she will be responsible for the financial management of the project, both on a day-to-day basis and also in the long term. The ability to draw up budgets, monitor and predict spending and present concise, realistic financial reports to each committee meeting is important.

These four officer posts are all crucial to the successful running of a scheme and all four people need to be in good, regular contact with one another.

If there are people on the committee who are skilled, experienced and willing to fill these posts, all the better. If not, people should not be afraid to take up such positions because of inexperience. If people are prepared to work from a base of enthusiasm, that is a good enough platform to start on. With experience, and support from other committee members, confidence will grow.

It is always worth looking out for management training run by local Voluntary Service Agencies, who often do one-day or weekend workshops on how to run committees and what the role and function of committee officers are. There are also leaflets, pamphlets and books on the subject from organisations such as the National Council for Voluntary Organisations. We suggest getting hold of some of these.

In our work we have met a marked lack of enthusiasm from a number of voluntary management committees to participate in training events, with comments like, 'What do we need training for?' or, 'We know what we're doing, we don't need help'. We feel this is short-sighted and naive and perhaps reveals an insecurity in some people about being exposed to new ideas and methods. It is quite imperative in our view that management people, like staff, take such opportunities as are available to pick up new ideas on how committees function and also develop skills for analysing and focusing on the purpose – aims and objectives – of their work.

We have come across a number of groups who have been caught up in a trap of continual dispute over such issues as the relationship between management and staff, the role of the chairperson or secretary, resentment of the views held by other committee members, and the fear of some people to express their views because they might be belittled. All of these can lead to the stagnation of a project, yet can be worked on and resolved if training opportunities are taken up. (We are not suggesting that management committee members need to acquire all the training of full-time professionals, but we do feel it is important that they have the opportunity to develop their insight into what they are doing.)

A committee is not just made up of four officers; there have to be other members who have a role and function to perform. Their background and experience will determine what they have to offer but each must be valued and respected for their contribution. All must feel part of the committee and its work, and able to participate; this is where the skills of the officers, and in particular the chairperson, come in. If people feel their skills are not valued they will leave, or become passive and frustrated members of the committee. Our experience has shown this again and again. One project committee invited a powerful and skilled deputy head of a special school to join it. She did, but after several meetings found that the group ignored her expertise and did not value the contributions she made. She left, rather angry and frustrated, and took her skills elsewhere.

Having outlined these basic points, we should point out that, no matter how well constituted – in both senses of the word – a committee may be, disagreement and debate will, and should, occur. It is the nature of all groups that conflict exists and it would be unhealthy if it did not. The difference, as far as we are concerned, is that the skilled, aware group can deal with conflict and still carry out its work positively. The uninformed, less self-aware group cannot and will not deal with disagreement and dissension, and this will reflect on the running of the project; in particular, it will be reflected through the attitude of staff, who find nothing more frustrating than an incompetent management group.

The final issue important to remember at this stage is that management committees must not become dominated by one or two people, either in terms of personality or of workload. A committee is a group, and jobs and responsibility must be shared out. Quite simply, one or two people can not adequately carry out all the tasks that need to be done. If they try to, some jobs will be done inadequately and time will be wasted as a result. A committee is, by its constitution, a democratic body and should operate accordingly.

Funding

Funding is also looked at in Chapter 6; we deal here with the aspects of it that relate specifically to the early stages of a new project.

Having established a need and created a management group, one of the first tasks must be to identify sources of money and develop a fund-raising strategy. We would suggest as a first stage that a new committee establishes a fund-raising sub-group. This could be convened by the Treasurer, although such does not have to be the case. The sub-group should contain people who have fund-raising contacts and experience, and above all people who are enthusiastic and positive about the task of raising money. The group need not be made up entirely of full management committee members; outside people can be brought in. Indeed, some people will only be willing to serve on the fund-raising committee, and will not be interested in wider management responsibilities. This group would meet between general committee meetings and report back to the main management body. The creation of this fund-raising sub-group should not take away from the main committee the responsibility of finding resources. Essentially, what the sub-group should aim for is to develop a campaign and lay basic plans in which everyone participates.

The fund-raising strategy should revolve around three areas of work. Firstly, exploring Central Government funding (such as Urban Aid grants or Inner City Partnership schemes), and local and health authority funding. For both central and local authority funding you will have to go through the local government or health service network. This is where having the experience and support of local authority officers and elected officials on the management group becomes invaluable. They will advise on how, where and when to apply. It is our experience that applications which are badly phrased, or are submitted at the wrong time, are invariably dismissed. If this happens, a group may well gain a bad reputation for shoddily presented grant applications, which may affect their future prospects for financial support.

The second area to explore is that of grants from trusts, industry and commerce. Consult the *Directory of Grant-Making Trusts*, often found in libraries, and see what trusts would be interested in disability and children. Then write to them for further information. There may well be local, as well as national, trusts to whom you could apply who would be prepared to support you. For example, Jonathan Page playground in Aylesbury, Buckinghamshire, is supported by the local Harding Educational Foundation, and the Hayward playground in North London has a substantial amount of their capital costs donated by the Hayward Foundation.

As far as industry and commerce is concerned, the task is to identify who operates locally. Insurance companies, building societies, banks, factories and other industrial concerns should all be approached, not just by letter but by personal contact as well. It may be that such organisations will offer one-off grants, or 'adopt' the project for several months or even a year. The Handicapped Adventure Playground Association, for instance, was adopted as Marks and Spencer's 'Charity of the Year' in 1979, and thousands of pounds were raised.

Do not 'soak' all these contacts at once: work through them methodically. Remember that at this stage you are looking for money to start the project. You will need revenue money coming in after it has started, and if you have exhausted all local contacts it will be that much more difficult to continue to raise funds. This is why we deliberately use the term fund-raising *strategy*.

It is important when approaching industry and commerce to go in and offer a variety of ways in which they could help you. Do not just ask for a straight grant or donation. Companies, and indeed trusts, are more likely to help if they know they will get some publicity, as, for example, if you offer to name the building after them. At the Chelsea Handicapped Adventure Playground the inside of the building was called the 'Violet Melchett Room', after the trust that donated money to the project. Another way in which a number of projects and business interests have both benefited is by window displays going up in building societies or banks, with collecting boxes inside, combined with the company itself offering a donation. Offering to put plaques up in buildings is another way of attracting sponsorship.

When applying for grants and donations from businesses and trusts, always be specific about what the money will be used for: fencing, playhut, outdoor play structures, mobile play equipment, salaries . . . Sponsors like to know exactly what their money is going towards. When actually at meetings present people with a list of costed items that they can consider, ranging from cheaper equipment such as toys and games to more expensive items like staff salaries. This is a useful method to employ, not just when setting up a playground but also once it is running.

What local authorities, trusts and business people will also want to see from a group making application to them is a set of financial plans. It is therefore essential to work out a detailed budget of proposed costs. In the early stages, before a playground is running, a detailed budget is obviously difficult to construct, but a basic target figure can be set with estimates of individual costs given within that target. Such a plan shows that thought has been put into the scheme and will impress potential sponsors. Your first estimated figures should be drawn up even before you have finalised your choice of site and building plans. Drawing up a budget is also a useful exercise for the management committee, as it gives them a chance to see what they should realistically be aiming for in terms of money. As a project matures it will hold Annual General Meetings where financial statements will have to be produced. Usually groups can, from such statements, draw up spending plans for the coming year.

The third area that the fund-raising group needs to consider is that of its own fund-raising activities. These range from summer fairs to sponsored walks, raffles to jumble sales. They are all labour-intensive efforts and if not properly organised are, quite frankly, not worth the effort. A jumble sale, for instance, needs at least 10–12 people to help collect and sell the jumble and publicise the sale; this involves spending time putting the event together. If it raises £30–40 is it all worth it? Could not that time and energy have been better spent drafting out a trust application or talking to a local businessperson?

A well-organised fair or sponsored event, however, could raise several hundreds, if not several thousands, of pounds. The other advantage of an event like this is that it also attracts publicity. If successful, such occasions also raise the morale of a committee quite considerably. Plan your own fund-raising efforts carefully, so that, for instance, your sponsored event does not clash with another going on locally. Do not exhaust yourselves by relying solely on your own events, because they will never raise all the resources you need. A couple of major fund-raising activities per year, plus participation in joint Christmas or summer fairs, is all that you should reasonably be expected to achieve.

When organising your own events, a rich source of support can often be found in local Round Table, Rotary and Lions clubs. Indeed, these are good organisations to be sponsored by for a period of time, and are also a possible source of contacts in the business and local government worlds. We would strongly suggest that a member of one or several of these bodies be brought on to the fund-raising group at an early stage.

Finally, it is only right for us to point out that getting adequate money to set up a project and then run it is a long task which will need to continue for as long as you want the project to stay open. It is important to realise this. Money, particularly in today's financial climate, only comes through dogged hard work. The message we give to people starting up is: plan your strategy, work hard and determinedly, view your work in the long term, be patient and remain enthusiastic!

A Site

While you are starting to look for funds you should also begin to identify sites. You may already have a piece of land in mind – perhaps that is what has started the whole idea of setting up a project. But if that is not the case, you will need to find out what exists. Local authorities are the first people to contact for help. If they can not help directly they should be able to guide you to people and places who can. Sites vary in shape, size and makeup and none are identical. An ideal size would be one to one and a half acres, but some projects exist successfully on smaller sites, while some are even larger.

The outdoor area of a playground needs to contain a number of elements to make it viable as a working site. Good drainage is a mundane but essential example of this. If a site is boggy it will be most difficult to build structures, maintain a sand pit and generally conserve good grassy play surfaces on which activities ranging from sitting and eating lunch to ball games can take place. A continuous muddy surface does not provide a good play area. If the natural drainage is inadequate, land drains will have to be installed.

A feature of all adventure playgrounds for handicapped children is the presence not only of grass surfaces but of trees and bushes as well. These natural growths often provide character and atmosphere to outdoor sites, particularly if the trees are mature. At Fulham Palace playground the blossom on some of their trees in springtime adds enormously to the colour and ambience of the site. At Jonathan Page playground in Aylesbury, the whole site is full of trees and tangled bushes which give that playground a unique and exciting atmosphere. It is possible to plant trees and quick-growing bushes and hedges if none exist, but they will need some protection in the early stages. Where there is little grass it is worth replanting with turf. Again, this needs time to settle.

A naturally undulating site also provides interest and stimulation. Some flat areas are needed, on which to build play structures, sand pits and a pond, but slopes provide added interest and challenge, and make possible such features as a slide down the side of a mound.

If a site does not contain natural raised features they can be built in. This is quite a major task and ought not to be underestimated. A mound is not just created by heaping earth together. It has to be carefully constructed, with the ground on which it will be sitting prepared and the mound built up in stages, with attention being paid to internal drainage. It should then be turfed and allowed to settle for some 5–6 months before it is used for play purposes. A badly-built mound will slip and cause untold problems, and become in the end a part of the playground that can not safely be used. We advise great caution in building these features: it is not something you should do without professional advice.

The next element to consider is how to fence the site. Are there any boundaries already in place, such as existing walls? There is no doubt that if you find a site with existing boundaries it will save considerable money, as good fencing, which you must have, can be expensive. If a site is not already fenced you will have to negotiate the boundaries. Do this with an eye to the natural features of the land, especially trees. If this produces a weirdly-shaped site do not worry; projects should not necessarily have to be square or rectangular: an unusually shaped site will contribute to your playground's individual character.

The type of fencing will depend on where you are situated. Low wooden fences might be suitable in, for instance, a residential setting such as the grounds of a long-stay hospital, but in a more community-based environment tougher fencing will be necessary. We do not recommend chain link, which is easy to climb, can often become bent and distorted and looks unattractive for a playground. Strong wooden fencing is preferable, up to about eight foot. Do not enclose the site completely as it is important for children to be able to see out and passers-by to see in. Remember that people living nearby might find it highly undesirable to see a completely enclosed area. Wooden fencing can look attractive from both inside and outside. Incorporated into the fence there needs to be a lockable main entrance and exit.

Good access is important. When children arrive an adequate entrance area on to the site is necessary and needs to be planned for. Children will often arrive by mini-bus and sometimes by coach, so they need to disgorge safely into the playground and not on to a busy road or pavement. Remember that parked cars can prevent vehicles drawing up to deliver children; you may need to contact your local Highways Department and ask them to ban parking on the relevant area outside your gates. (A friendly local councillor may come in very handy here!)

Once on site, good access around it is necessary, particularly for children who are in wheelchairs or who have other mobility problems. This means planning out a system of paths, which does not need to be elaborate but should give basic access to most parts of the site. Paths also ensure that go-karts and other wheeled equipment can be used, and make it possible to use the site when the ground is wet and muddy. We recommend tarmac paths rather than concrete, even though these are more expensive. Tarmac, if properly rolled, is a softer, less abrasive surface than concrete. Paths need to be wide enough for two wheelchairs to pass one another. The starting place for paths should be the main site entrance and the exits from the play building.

It is useful, though not essential, at this early stage of looking at a site, to determine where a pond and sand pit might be located. These are two important elements of the outdoor area.

A pond obviously has to be filled and periodically drained, so its location may well be determined by the layout of the existing drainage system. Many playground ponds have been difficult to maintain properly because of poor drainage that has been built in: a great deal of thought needs to go into how the pond is constructed. Apart from fencing, a pond – including a pump, filter system and drains – could be the most expensive item on the outdoor site, possibly costing £6–7,000 (1984 figures). We recommend visiting projects that have ponds, discussing with the people there what the pitfalls are and learning from their experience.

A playground pond does not need to be deep – and indeed might be a hazard if it were. The two most popular activities in such ponds are paddling and water fights. We particularly favour the type of design that includes an artificial stream, thus increasing the variety of ways that children can use it and also making possible the building-in of bridges as described by Lady Allen:

> A bridge is fun to cross over or throw things in from, or simply to sit and watch from. It is also interesting to paddle through underneath, or to sail under on a homemade raft or boat, so a bridge should be built high enough above the water for these purposes, while care is taken to make it accessible for everyone.

The sand pit is less of a problem, although it does have to be built in such a way that it, too, drains adequately. Sand pits should have a maximum depth of three feet, but be quite large in area. Ideally, they should be walled from the base up to six inches or a foot above ground level. This stops a lot of sand being spread outside the pit and also provides useful seating for some children. The foundations should have basic drainage. A simple method is to lay a crazy paving pattern of pavement blocks with gaps between them so that water can drain through the sand and then through the gaps in the blocks and into the earth.

Having sand and water adjacent, like a beach, is attractive to children, but they should not be put too close together. A gap of at least five or six feet is necessary. A number of playgrounds have found that, if large amounts of sand get into the pond, the water very quickly becomes dirty, the drainage and filter systems get blocked and damaged and a lot of time has to be spent in cleaning and maintaining them.

When looking at a site and envisaging where the paths, fencing, pond and sand pit might go, as well as taking the trees and bushes into account, consider what space there is for play structures, because these are a fundamental part of the playground and cannot be left out. Do *not* plan your climbing frames, slides, swings and runways – they can develop at a later date – but do make sure that there is space for them to be built.

Flat areas also need to be considered for such activities as ball games, barbecues and use of inflatables. Ideally, these should be grassed, although hard-surface areas for ball games can be used. Park View playground in Knowsley, Liverpool, and the Thames Valley playground near Maidenhead have hard-surface ball game areas which were financed by the Goaldiggers Trust, who offer grants for such developments. It is imperative, however, when using inflatables, to have them on grass areas. Then, a child who slips off will be unhurt, whereas a fall on to tarmac or concrete could result in nasty scratches or bruises.

When looking at a site, the most fundamental decision is where to place the playhut and what size the building will be. Basically, its position will depend on the nature of the land and how large it needs to be. So, for example, it cannot be constructed where there are mature trees. It also needs to be in such a position as to give a clear view of the site, so that staff can see from the building what is happening in the rest of the playground. The playhut is the single most expensive capital item of a playground. A minimum target for building such a facility is £40–50,000 (1984 figures).

The site you have in mind may already be attached to a building such as a community centre or church hall. The playhut at Park View playground is based in a former day nursery. You will save considerable expense if you can operate from within an existing facility, or a disused one. It would be right to point out, however, that operating from within an already used building could cause considerable conflict. For instance, if a playground shares a building with a community centre, many of the indoor play activities could disrupt old folk's clubs or other more formal events. A purpose-built indoor play area within such a centre, with its own access to the outdoor site, might overcome this problem. There is no doubt that a vacant building, as in Park View's case, is a good option if it adjoins a suitable open space.

If the site has no building then one obviously has to be constructed. We do not intend to go into all the different types of playhut that exist, but again recommend that visits be made to existing projects to see buildings in operation. You will need to employ an architect to design your building. Try to find one who already has experience of designing for people with disabilities or children. Above all, try to find a firm prepared to work closely in consultation with your committee. Make sure they visit existing projects with you so that they can see the design issues at first hand, and can discuss their proposals with experienced playworkers. It is highly unlikely that they will previously have designed any building that suffers such rough usage as a play building, and it will be easy for them to underestimate the need for robust fixtures and attention to the particular safety considerations made necessary by the way adventure playgrounds are used.

A number of different factors must be taken into account in planning a building, whether purpose-built or already in existence. The particular reasons given by the Handicapped Adventure Playground Association for having a play building are: to provide shelter and warmth in cold or wet weather; to house lavatories, washing facilities and drying rooms; to provide adequate storage space, work room, art area, cooking facilities and office accommodation.

The centre of such a facility is the play room itself, in which there should be a craft area with sink, space for indoor play structures such as a small slide, a quiet corner with books and space for a variety of games and toys. It is useful to decide the location of the art area, as this will always be a popular, thriving activity which will need a substantial amount of space and good – preferably natural – lighting.

Near the play area there must be an office with a telephone and enough space for a desk and filing cabinet. The first aid kit will be housed in here. It is ideal if the office can look out on both the outside site and the indoor area, so that when workers find themselves on the phone, or doing some urgent administrative work, they can do this with one eye on the activities going on elsewhere.

A kitchen is a must. Drinks have to be made, during holiday periods food often has to be prepared for children, and above all the children who use such playgrounds do enjoy cooking. If it is a wet or cold day, for instance, cooking indoors makes a good substitute for outside play. The kitchen needs to have space enough for several wheelchairs, surfaces at various heights, large sinks and draining boards and plenty of shelving. A fridge/ freezer and cooker are essential. Hatchways looking out on to the main indoor play area make the kitchen feel part of the overall play space.

Lavatories and washing facilities are essential. There must be an absolute minimum of two toilets, preferably four or five. Several of these need to be adapted for wheelchair users. Wash basins are needed: remember the height of these for wheelchair children. A shower is important as well, both for children who get very wet and dirty while playing, and for incontinent children who may need cleaning. A shower is also useful for staff to clean up at the end of a day's work. It is sensible to have drawers or cupboards fitted to house spare clothes and incontinence pads, plus space for the wellies and wetsuits that children may wear for playing in the pond. A collapsible surface on which to sit or lie children while cleaning them or changing clothes is also useful. Experience has shown that it is really worthwhile to plan this area carefully.

Attached to the lavatories, there needs to be a small area where clothes and towels can be washed and dried. This should include a washing machine and tumble drier. A staff lavatory and changing room is also necessary for playground workers and visiting adults. This need not be large, but should contain secure lockers in which valuables can be placed.

The final necessary facility within a playhut is good storage space. This ranges from shelving around the side of the play area to storage rooms in which tools, paint, mobile vehicles and general equipment can be kept. It is a fact that no playground yet built has enough storage space. Indeed, as a project grows, more and more materials come on to site and need to be housed. We stress the importance of this because potential play space is often taken up with equipment which is not in use, and because badly stored materials are often easily damaged. If possible, a work bench within a store room is a good idea so that equipment can be mended on it, although this is not absolutely necessary if space is at a premium.

Good strong floor surfaces are necessary everywhere around a play building. They need to be resistant to dirt, water, grit and general heavy use, and easy to clean. In the kitchen, lavatories and laundry room we would recommend tiling, as this type of flooring is easily cleaned. In the rest of the building a tough, durable surface is vital. It is worth spending several thousand pounds on a good floor. Projects that have laid cheaper, or unsuitable, flooring have come to regret it. At Chelsea and Fulham Palace playgrounds cork floor was laid. It proved to be totally unsuitable, for after the varnish had worn off the top of the cork through use, water and dirt got into the material, destroyed the glue and eventually lifted the floor.

Heating also has to be carefully thought out. Many common forms of heating, including radiators, stoves and electric or gas fires, could be dangerous to children using a playground. We consider ducted hot air, pushed out at ground level, as suitable. Again, this can be an expensive item to instal and it is important to get it right first time.

Two other points need mentioning in relation to the building. The first is access. There should be a main entrance large enough to contain the flow of people in and out and wide enough for two wheelchairs to pass. Other doorways must also be wide enough for a wheelchair to pass through. Try to eliminate all steps in buildings. If this proves difficult, build a ramp beside the step or over the step.

Secondly, in designing a building, make sure it is bright inside, since a hut that is dark often feels claustrophobic. This means having plenty of windows, and possibly roof lights, and placing the building in such a way that it is not permanently shrouded in shadow. It also saves considerable electricity costs. Several existing play buildings have to have their lights on constantly because they are too dark, even during the summer months.

In looking at a site that might be suitable, always try to get a survey plan so that you can discover whether there are underground cables, pipes or old foundations, which may hamper construction. Charlie Chaplin playground had to revise its plans at a late stage after discovering a large gas pipe, and numerous playgrounds have unearthed telephone cables, land drainage features and old foundations. Plans should be available from the local authority.

Obviously, when a piece of land has been found a lease or licence will have to be negotiated with the owner. For voluntary organisations this can usually be done at a peppercorn rent. For projects within residential establishments, there may be no cost at all if the facility is directly serving the hospital or home. Make sure that as secure a base as possible is gained. Do not find yourselves in the position of Chelsea playground, which had to close, amid much publicity, due to the ending at short notice of its lease arrangement. Most potential funding bodies will not give money to a project which has not got a site with a secure lease.

Finally, it is appropriate to mention vandalism. Every site is susceptible to damage and no site can be designed or built to stop it entirely. Those two facts have to be faced. What it does mean, of course, is that outdoor structures must be securely built, and where feasible outdoor play equipment such as ropes and go-karts should be securely stored inside the building at night. A strong fence and main gate are also necessary. The building must have solid doors with strong locks. Windows and doors may need shutters that are brought down at night. Make sure all internal doors are securely built and lockable. Consider installing a security alarm in the building. Bad vandalism such as the fire that burnt out a great deal of the Lady Allen playground building in November 1983 can be avoided if such measures are taken. It is worth spending extra money to make a site secure in this way; doing so will also reduce your insurance premium.

Publicity

Publicity goes hand in hand with fund-raising but does require a separate mention. From the early days it is useful to have a leaflet to give to people. This can be handed out at meetings, included in grant applications and distributed at fairs and other events. It should contain basic information on the scheme and offer suggestions on how people can help. As the project opens a new leaflet can be designed giving more specific details, with photographs of the playground in use.

A regular free news-sheet is also a good idea to keep people up to date with how things are progressing, implanting in their minds the awareness that such a playground will soon be in existence. Continue the news-sheet once the project is open. The Gloucestershire Adventure Playground, near Cheltenham, adopted this method of publicising their work.

The local press is always worth using: for advertising events, appealing for equipment and doing regular articles on how the scheme is developing. Striking up a good relationship with one or two journalists is often profitable and can lead to more prominent articles. The East London Handicapped Adventure Playground, for example, had some equipment badly vandalised in January 1984, got the incident publicised in the local press and received money from numerous donations which exceeded the cost of the vandalism.

Local radio and television are also possible channels to use, although they are more likely to be interested when the project opens. If you get a well-known personality to come along it may help to arouse their interest.

Publicity of a different sort can be gained from attending relevant meetings and conferences such as local play association meetings and training events, and talking about the project either formally or informally. If your face is seen regularly, people will identify you with the project and ask about progress and development. This approach is invaluable in the long run, as it gains support and credibility for the scheme. As your project develops, you will find that you need to liaise with some of these other organisations; it will be much easier to do so if you have already struck up a good relationship with them.

Let it be known that there are members of the committee, or perhaps outside speakers, who are prepared to come and talk to meetings ranging from school assemblies to Rotary dinners.

It is always a good idea near the beginning of a project to organise a public meeting and invite as wide an audience as possible, including the Lord Mayor. Invite the press and have several speakers with a film and slides. The purpose of this is publicly to launch the playground and make clear to all what you wish to achieve. Use it to appeal for funds, material help, volunteers and committee members, and above all to show that you are serious in your intent. Hold another meeting nearer the opening date of the playground and show what progress is being made. Hold an opening ceremony on the actual site when it is about to start to receive children.

Having plans and models available for show is useful. These can be used at meetings and talks and, of course, are good to have to show potential sponsors and donors. They add a visual image to the talk. Putting these up as a display in a local library or the town hall for several weeks is a constructive way of informing local people about the playground and asking for their support.

Publicity and public relations, like fund raising, is a constant activity which should never come to an end. Always look for new and inventive ways of gaining press coverage that will benefit the project, not just in the run-up to getting it established but in the long term as well.

Transport
Transport is mentioned here because the vast majority of children will not be able to get to the playground without

assistance. Many schools and hospitals have minibuses which can transport children to and from the project, but some may not. Similarly, a number of individual children who could use the scheme during holidays and at weekends may not have transport available. It is important to consider seriously what transport is around, for there is quite simply no point in having a playground if people cannot get to it.

It is perhaps necessary to consider purchasing a minibus for the project if it appears that many potential users will not be able to get there without such assistance. The East London Handicapped Adventure Playground and Park View playground are two projects that have done this, with the aid of minibuses donated by the Variety Club of Great Britain. Otherwise, it may be worthwhile to see if another local voluntary organisation, such as MENCAP, can loan its minibus on particular days when the project needs it. Local authority transport may also be available, although this will be more difficult to come by. It is best to put in specific requests for specific days to secure this type of commitment. Another method, particularly during the holiday periods, is to persuade parents to bring several children in their car rather than just their own child.

We do urge committees to consider this issue in the planning stages and explore with all the relevant people – schools, local authority, hospitals, residential homes, other voluntary organisations and parents – what is available and how it can best be organised to get maximum use of the playground. (A useful credential for playstaff is to be able to drive.)

Staffing

How a project is to be staffed must be considered from the early days. An adventure playground is a full-time project requiring full-time personnel. You cannot successfully run the kind of project we are talking about in this book without this provision. We recommend an absolute minimum of two full-timers supplemented by voluntary and/or part-time workers. If you can possibly raise the funding, you should have at least four full-time playworkers. This is the minimum number that will enable you to be reasonably sure of having a minimum of two workers on site at any given time: do not forget that you have to make allowance for holidays, sickness, time off in lieu and work done off-site, such as buying supplies and visiting organisations that use the playground.

Staff provide the energy and initiative that a playground needs to be a successful and exciting place for children. They are also needed to maintain the site and make sure it is safe to use. Another important function is to maintain and develop community contacts with schools, parents, hospitals and other voluntary organisations. This is a role that can be shared with committee members. Playworkers are the pivotal link that makes a playground tick for visiting staff and parents, the management committee and above all the children.

There is no doubt that the job of the playworker is an exhausting one, requiring considerable commitment and a variety of skills. One of the best descriptions of the qualities needed to be a playworker is a Robin Hood type of character possessing energy, adaptability, practical skills, the ability to relate to many different people, to act on the spur of the moment and have a sense of humour! There is no doubt that a good playworker is the most valuable and worthwhile asset to a scheme and should be seen in such a light by management.

Because staff are crucial, try to secure the best possible salaries for them. This can be difficult, but the better the salary the broader the range of people who might apply for the post, thus giving a better selection of people to choose from. Do not operate on the principle that it is a 'worthwhile' job to do, and people have to be 'dedicated' to work in this field. Such an approach leads to justifying the payment of low salaries and affording staff a lower status than other workers such as teachers. A good playworker is as invaluable as a good teacher.

Apart from the initial capital outlay in developing a playground, staff salaries will become the single most costly item of revenue expenditure, and again this needs to be recognised and planned for. So, when applying for grants or donations, make sure that staff salaries are very close to the top of your 'shopping list', along with building or site development costs.

Staff need support, particularly if a project can only employ two people and the playground is in an isolated geographical setting without access to other play workers or play organisations. Management committees must be aware of this from the beginning and offer staff the opportunity to talk about their work and the feelings and ideas it arouses. Many committees are very bad at this; they leave their staff to 'sink or swim' and then get angry when playworkers turn round and seem to rebuff the management for the work it is doing. Make it clear from the beginning that the committee is willing to act as a support service to workers. This is an example of how some basic training for management committee members could come in useful. Staff themselves should have access to in-service training opportunities. (This is pursued in more depth in Chapter 4.)

We strongly recommend employing a playworker as soon as possible, certainly before the project is open to children. This enables the worker to become familiar with the site and its potential, meet prospective users (such as schools and hospital groups), make him- or herself known in the community, and of course get used to working with the management group. He or she can start to plan the playground timetable, order equipment and help in the last stages of building up the whole site. If workers have been involved with this for several months before the children arrive, they will be much more prepared and ready to offer a service than if they are employed a few days before the gates open. Experience has shown that this is by far the best way of going about employing your first staff.

It is important to get the right staff at the beginning of a scheme. They will lead it off and need to establish it as an important and valued facility. Many eyes will be on them, not least those of the management committee who have put in the hard work of developing the project from dream to reality. The criteria for good playworkers are described in another chapter, but it is worth scouring long and hard, and perhaps having several sets of interviews before a final decision is made. Regard this appointment as fundamental to the project's successful development.

Full-time staffing will need to be supplemented by volunteer or part-time workers – employing a cleaner, for instance, or extra workers for the busy summer holiday period. Bear this in mind and have some money put aside for this purpose. It is always worth paying the travelling expenses of a good, reliable volunteer. Do not think, however, that such workers can substitute for full-time staff. They cannot, and should not be expected to try.

In conclusion, it is worth pointing out that management committee responsibilities change when staff are employed. For several years before staff come along, a committee will have got used to working for itself. By employing workers it takes on a new role, that of employer, and it is important to recognise this change. Some committees have failed to realise this and carried on in their former ways, almost ignoring their duty to their staff. This has invariably led to conflict. Committee attitudes towards workers are often clearly reflected through job descriptions, salaries and contracts. Committees must seriously consider their role as employers – for example, by becoming familiar with employment legislation – and realise from this that their responsibilities have changed: they have entered a new phase in their own development.

Equipment

Having advanced well along the road to establishing a playground, it is useful to start planning and looking for the equipment that will be necessary once it is running. A lot of this should be included in your 'shopping list' of items that can be sponsored, but not all of it can be expected to arrive in this way. For instance, wood for building play structures is an item that you will probably have to buy or scrounge, whereas adapted tricycles or go-karts, for example, may be sponsored.

A playground survives on all kinds of equipment, ranging from yoghurt cartons and loo rolls to washing machines and minibuses, so be on the lookout several months before the scheme opens. Second-hand armchairs, desks, filing cabinets, shelves, tables, bicycles, games, books, saucepans, paintbrushes and dressing-up clothes are all usable on a playground and can save money. Do not feel that every piece of equipment has to be new; part of the fun of these projects is the re-using and recycling of apparently abandoned objects.

All statutory authorities have supplies depots which a playground may be able to use; most of the London playgrounds use the GLC Supply Depots. Materials such as tools are often cheaper here than in shops, and can be bought in bulk where appropriate. This is a useful way of purchasing goods, and ensures that there is more than one hammer or light bulb available, should one break. Alternatively, you might be able to negotiate a discount with a local shop if you buy all your tools, nails, paint, electrical items and so on there.

The best way of finding out what equipment a project needs is to go through each area, such as kitchen, office, playroom, sand pit, and draw up a list of necessary items. Isolate those that can be got secondhand or through scrounging, and leave yourself with a list of goods that you need to purchase or have donated. Circularise your scrounging list to as many people as possible. This is a good system to keep going once the playground is open, because projects always need a vast range of resources and materials coming in.

The planning stages of a playground, from the first idea to its opening, involve hard work, commitment and patience on the part of at least eight to ten people. Dr Charles Pocock from the Basildon Project again:

> The process of establishing an adventure playground for handicapped children – from the germ of an idea to final fruition – is often fraught with quite enormous problems, not the least of which is obtaining a suitable site and the necessary money to finance the project.

Do not, however, let this put you off the idea of setting up a playground: let it, instead, serve to remind you that to do so takes time. Don't expect over-rapid results and then get despondent when difficulties arise. Keep going, because the end result is an exceptionally worthwhile one. We believe, based on our own personal experience, that if you are determined, and believe strongly enough in the concept of adventure play, then you will succeed. We can guarantee that, once you see *your* playground in operation, you will be sure it was worth all the effort put into establishing it.

4 Playwork

An adventure playground's most important resource is its playworkers; the success of any project of the sort we describe in this book is absolutely dependent on the abilities of a team of competent and experienced play staff. While one can point to various necessary attributes, such as energy, dedication, awareness, sensitivity, intuitiveness, enthusiasm, patience, a sense of humour and the ability to get on with other people, the skills that are needed to carry out this unique and demanding job need to be defined more precisely. It is partly because many people, including some playworkers and management, find it difficult to state what a playworker's role consists of, that the job is often viewed with a mixture of amused condescension, hostility and amazement by other professionals, parents and some users. If such people were more familiar with playground work, they would realise that it consists of far more than just 'getting on with children': a good playworker needs a wide range of specific skills and knowledge, backed by a good theoretical understanding of the nature of her task.

Appointing Staff

The first step in creating a team of playworkers is to appoint the right people. This is particularly important for a new playground, where it is not simply a matter of finding a single person to fit in with an existing team and contribute to a set of activities that has already been established, but of putting together a group of people who will work well together. The choice of a team of workers is effectively a decision about the nature of the playground and its activities. Interviewing panels should be aware that, in appointing individuals with particular skills or areas of interest, they are making decisions about the playground's future which they must be prepared to follow up. Workers who feel that they are being prevented from making a full contribution to the playground's activities because their management committee will not provide appropriate resources to let them use their skills are likely to become justifiably resentful, which is very bad for playground morale.

It is advisable to advertise as widely as possible, so that a good range of applicants is attracted, and this should be budgeted for when planning a new project. In particular, job vacancies should be made known to other play projects and organisations, to try to attract people who are already experienced in play work. Advertisements should contain the job title and basic details of employment conditions such as salary and holiday allowance. These should be supplemented by a full job description sent out with the application form; in drawing these up, it can be useful to consult other projects and get copies of their job descriptions to use as a basic guide. Application forms should be long and thorough enough to enable applicants to respond fully.

When shortlisting applicants, bear in mind that good playworkers come from an enormous range of backgrounds, and their capacity for working with children may not, if they have no previous playground experience, be represented by paper qualifications: some of the best playworkers we know have no formal qualifications whatsoever; in such cases, an interviewing panel ought to be able to recognise that a natural aptitude for relating to children (even where the panel has to read between the lines of a nervous interviewee's words to recognise it) combined with experience of working on playgrounds, is the best possible qualification.

It is worth inviting shortlisted applicants to visit the playground before their interview, so that they can see the scheme and gain a clearer idea of what the job involves. The combination of an informal visit, with an opportunity to talk to existing workers or committee members, and a more formal interview makes the task of selecting the right worker easier, and gives the job applicants a better opportunity to show themselves and explain at the interview how they might contribute to the project.

An interview panel should not normally consist of more than four or five people; a larger number is likely to be too intimidating for the interviewees. If the playground is a new one, with an inexperienced committee appointing its first staff, the panel should, if at all possible, include at least one person who has experience of working on, or managing, a playground. This will help ensure that the appropriate questions get asked, and will also help in the summing-up discussion at the end of each interview and in making the final decision. It is also good practice to discuss beforehand what questions should be asked and by whom. Applicants should also be given an opportunity to ask their own questions about the project, and should be given full and clear details about the potential conditions of service so that they know exactly where they stand.

The most obvious questions that need to be asked concern a person's experience in the areas of play and disability. It is rare for applicants to have backgrounds in both, and we feel that it is more important for them to have knowledge of adventure play than of disability. Expertise in working with people with disabilities can be picked up through contact, as part of the normal procedure of developing individual relationships with each child who uses the project, but competence at working in an adventure play setting is a particular skill with which many people may not feel comfortable. The ability to maintain high professional standards in all areas, from timekeeping and health and safety to interaction with severely disabled or disturbed children, within the informal and superficially unstructured environment of a playground, demands a level of self-discipline that is not called for in other, equally demanding but more formally structured, careers. Among other things, playwork demands a flexibility of approach, willingness to work varying and sometimes inconvenient hours, an ability to carry out practical tasks and close team work. Unless workers are at ease from the start with this method of working, the element of excitement and adventure that needs to be present in all playgrounds can easily give way to a more formalised atmosphere which is quite definitely not suitable for an adventure playground.

In saying this, we do not mean to belittle the knowledge and skills of those who have worked with people with disabilities, such as special school teachers and occupational therapists. It rapidly becomes apparent to experienced adventure play-workers who have little knowledge of disability that they must acquire particular skills, information and personal attitudes if they are to make a successful job of working on a play project with children with disabilities. We still feel, however, that experience of adventure play should be a more important consideration during interviews than similar knowledge and experience of disability. A combination of both is obviously ideal.

Once the final decision has been made, the successful candidate should be informed as soon as possible, and a starting date agreed upon. When informing a person that he or she has been offered the job, a contract of employment should be enclosed, which must contain the minimum statutory requirements for a contract; for details of these consult a lawyer or a copy of another organisation's contract for employees. The new worker should return the signed contract within three months.

Playwork Skills

It is often stated that an ability to relate to children and understand their needs is the playworker's most important attribute. This is undoubtedly true, but not entirely helpful: the same could be said of parents, teachers, child psychiatrists or Scout and Guide leaders. Work on an adventure playground demands particular additional capabilities which are deter-mined by the nature of adventure play itself.

An adventure playground provides an opportunity for children of all abilities to explore and experiment with the environment around them, through communication, touch, movement, sound and colour. This exploration goes beyond what is offered in a classroom, the home or a hospital setting, and is consequently an essentially educational experience as valid and important as those offered elsewhere. An adventure playground should recognise, and base its work on, the child's development through play, and accordingly offer him the widest access to play opportunities that it possibly can. The playworker's task is therefore to provide these opportunities and encourage the children's participation in them.

The most important skill in this context is communication. Playground work means constant interaction with children on both individual and group levels, and a worker must feel comfortable with both types of contact. Communication varies from discussion with users of a building project or proposed camping trip to comforting a child who has hurt himself in an accident. These might not seem exceptional skills, but they must operate within the atmosphere and philosophy of an adventure playground, which means that children should take part in making decisions about their activities and have the opportunity to give vent, through physical and verbal channels, to their thoughts and ideas – however outrageous some of them might be!

Skill in communication involves much more than straight verbal contact: sensitivity, an ability to motivate others to express themselves and humour. Skills such as these are important when relating to any person or group; when working with children with disabilities they are absolutely vital. For instance, a child with cerebral palsy may have plenty to say, but take longer to speak than other children, with words that appear slurred to able-bodied listeners, accompanied by extensive involuntary physical movements. Such a child will know from experience that people tend to ignore what she is saying, cut her off before she has finished or try to complete what she is saying in order to avoid embarrassment or speed up the conversation. She should be able to feel confident that the playground is one place where she will be listened to attentively, by people who want to hear what she has to say.

Similarly, communicating with an autistic child who has little or no verbal speech but is trying to convey a need to the worker can cause some frustration and annoyance to the member of staff if she is not aware or tolerant enough of that child's communication needs. Such examples might seem to imply that the adventure play concept is difficult to convey or work with in relation to children with disabilities. This is not so. What is required is a heightened sensitivity to how communication can take place, coupled with a determination that it should, so that children with disabilities feel that they have a genuine voice on a playground.

The question of communication is closely interlinked with the ability to motivate children, which must be seen by playworkers as a very important part of their armoury of skills. Many children with disabilities have limited play experience, particularly of the adventurous type offered by a playground. When faced with such an opportunity, they may need help to meet the challenges it presents. This requires the playworker to encourage and prompt the child, and often show him how to go about a particular activity. It often takes considerable time, effort and patience on both the worker's and the child's side to do this, but such energy is well spent, as an example will demonstrate.

Robert is a severely mentally handicapped adolescent of eighteen who, if left to himself, will stand and rock backwards and forwards, humming and watching his fingers and hands in front of his eyes. It took many weeks to motivate him to take part in any activity, and this always needed a member of staff to take him by the hand and show him what to do. One particular play activity that he grew to enjoy was climbing up a set of stairs to the top of a slide and then going down the slide. Helping Robert to learn to do this was a long process, which had to be broken down into a series of separate stages. He first had to be encouraged to climb up stairs by holding on to the hand-rail and someone's arm, then to do it by himself, holding the rails with a member of staff encouraging him from the top, then to do it on his own with little or no encouragement. Having accomplished that much, he then had to get used to standing on a platform above ground and feeling safe. From there it was a matter of giving him confidence to go down a slide, something he had never experienced before. This was done by sitting him on a member of staff's lap and holding him as they went down the slide together. The next step involved having members of staff at the top and bottom of the slide as Robert came down. Eventually, it only needed one member of staff to help on the slide. At every stage encouragement was necessary, with Robert being congratulated and hugged when he had achieved certain goals. In the end he was able to carry out this activity virtually on his own, with great smiles and whoops as he came down the slide. It also meant that he often mixed in with other children, usually more able, who were also using the slide. This enabled him to enter into the give and take of sharing an experience with others – for instance, in waiting his turn to go down the slide.

There is no doubt that Robert would not have achieved, or even attempted, this without support. His success was dependent on the playground staff, who used their communication skills to motivate and perhaps even inspire him to do what he did.

A similar process of encouragement is used in getting children who are essentially wheelchair-bound on to go-karts, bicycles or other pieces of equipment, which feel far less familiar and secure than their chairs. This can take some gentle persuasion, encouragement and assurance that they will be safe, possibly backed up by the physical presence of a worker pushing or walking alongside. It may take some weeks to get such a child using the go-kart or bicycle independently; during all that time staff need to be on hand to prompt and assist.

Anybody who works on an adventure playground which is used by handicapped children must be prepared to put much of their energy into motivating many of the children who use the project. Without this, children such as Robert will be left to stand or sit on their own and indulge in repetitive obsessional behaviour and, if they get bored, possibly become disruptive or aggressive. Others may continue to play in a way in which they feel safe and secure, not exposing themselves to wider, more exciting activities which could help them develop new skills and view the world around them in a broader, more challenging light.

Sensitivity to children's needs is also important within communication. Staff must listen to children and be open to their ideas and suggestions, and must also be aware of the impact they as staff are having on children. Where, for instance, a successful relationship exists between a child and one particular member of staff, this should be recognised and a pattern of working developed that takes it into account. Such sensitivity is particularly important when working with children who have little or no verbal communication; like everybody else, they have preferences for certain people over others, but may not be able to make it so clear.

Sensitivity is equally necessary when disciplining children. Children with disabilities need to be disciplined as much as any other child, and the responsibility for doing so should not be shirked. It is, however, important to bear in mind such questions as to what extent the child knows it is doing wrong and whether the behaviour is the result of such factors as tension, frustration, anger or teasing; such information is particularly important if the child is a poor communicator, as are some autistic children. Other delicate decisions have to be made when the possibility exists that an action, such as a child soiling itself, is a ploy to gain attention; while such behaviour needs to be discouraged, a reprimand could be a thoroughly inappropriate response if the child's action is actually the result of some distress.

We cannot offer simple solutions to the issue of disciplining children, but do advise workers to talk to parents and teachers about the most appropriate methods and about the situations and feelings that spark off adverse behaviour in their children. We also advise staff to think very carefully about how, and why, they use particular methods of disciplining, and believe above all that it is important to be consistent in whatever approach is used.

The second most important skill when working in an adventure playground is, in our opinion, the ability to operate within a team setting, whether that team consists of two people or ten. This is clearly related to being the type of good communicator discussed above in relation to children. A playground can not offer the range of activities, stimulation, security and safeness it should unless the staff working on it are broadly agreed on their aims and objectives. This can only be achieved through discussion and debate. It is not good enough to adopt the laissez-faire approach of 'let it just happen'. Plans have to be made in relation to all such major areas as discipline, site development, maintenance work, policy towards difficult children and the purchase of goods and equipment. Everybody on the staff side needs to be involved in these discussions and make their thoughts known. Where this does not happen, unresolved conflicts, anger and confusion can result, which will inevitably spill over into the work done with children.

The staff as a group should also be able to offer support to individual members of the team, and be sensitive about when this is needed. Working in a playground can be an intense experience, particularly during holiday periods, and one which puts considerable pressure on workers. It is therefore important that there be an immediate forum, the staff team, to which they can refer for advice, information and guidance. Without this support staff can lose direction and confidence, by no means an uncommon event where workers do not act together. Where a playground has only a single worker, the lack of such support imposes a considerable extra strain on the worker.

One particular area where most playgrounds could benefit from greater mutual support is, ironically, that of disability. Few people have bodies that are in one hundred per cent working order, but we live in a society that puts great pressure on all but 'The Disabled' to live up to the assumption that they are completely able-bodied. Workers with severely disabled children or adults are particularly likely to feel 'what right have I got to make a fuss?' and keep their difficulties to themselves. This benefits nobody. We feel strongly that workers should be open with each other about their physcial limitations, so that each member of the playground team can give the others whatever support they may need. A playworker who has a bad back – the major occupational injury among playworkers – should feel able to ask for assistance in heavy lifting and other physical tasks; where a worker is vulnerable to hay fever, attempts should be made to arrange the distribution of duties so that her time is spent mainly indoors when the pollen count is high. It takes a certain amount of trust for workers to speak openly about their physical limitations and the kinds of support they need, but doing so reduces the pressures on each individual worker, lessens the likelihood of existing problems being aggravated (which, if it leads to that worker being off sick, would place extra strain on the other members of the team) and encourages a type of co-operation which is good for staff morale. Such an approach has the supplementary advantage that a team of workers who have faced up to the fact that they are not entirely able-bodied themselves are likely to have a changed attitude to the children with disabilities who use the playground.

A certain amount of formal structure is usually necessary to ensure the success of a team approach. There should, for instance, be a regular weekly team meeting, and a commitment from staff to discuss issues that might suddenly arise. On a play project for children with disabilities, it is important that the team discuss regularly whether the project is offering the right range of activities and working with the children in the most positive way possible. For instance, a playground might find that a group of autistic or severely mentally handicapped children are presenting a particular problem to the workers. The team would then need to consider such issues as whether too many children were coming at one time, so that not enough attention could be given to each of them, whether there was adequate communication between visiting school staff and playground staff, and whether the project was failing to offer the kind of activities and opportunities that these users would respond to. In such a case, the skills needed by the playground staff, both individually and as a team, include those of awareness, the ability to judge their own work and its effectiveness, a willingness to look at an issue from several viewpoints, the ability to admit to weakness as well as strength and a general commitment to discussing their work and its progress.

An important aspect of adventure play is progress through exploration and experimentation. This takes place between staff through discussion and debate. Without it, a project can stagnate, lose direction and forget the central reasons for its existence.

Staff need to possess a range of practical skills, or at least a capacity and willingness to pick them up. Bricklaying, woodworking, cooking, art and craft techniques, mechanical skills, first aid, scrounging, construction and design abilities and more are needed in a playground. No single individual can reasonably be expected to have all the skills that come in useful, but good playworkers will be continually expanding their basic skills through experience and training, especially where management attach adequate importance to creating training opportunities for their workers. It is useful, however, to have individual members of staff who are skilled in specific areas such as arts and crafts or mechanical and construction techniques. Those staff can impart their skills to others, and give a good range of activities to a project. (This raises the tricky issue of what balance to draw between taking advantage of individual expertise and sharing responsibilities as equally as possible; some examples of how this issue has been dealt with in industrial co-operatives can be found in Tony Gibson's *People Power*.) When staff appointments are being made, it is useful to look out for potential workers who have practical skills which may complement those already existing among the other members of the staff team.

The ability to adapt and experiment with practical skills is important, as with the use of scrap materials for craft activity (discussed further in the chapter on Resources), where there is enormous scope for development, particularly in relation to tactile experience, colour and fantasy play, as in the making of masks, puppets and models. The strongest example of this kind of activity that we have encountered is the annual Bonfire Night party held at Chelsea Adventure Playground. The staff, with everyone participating, build a huge guy, different each year, which has to date been a punk, a witch and a dragon, among other themes. It is built entirely out of scrap materials, ranging from large pieces of wood to milk bottle tops and bin liners. The creation of this expression of imaginative fantasy has involved children and adults in many different processes – not the least of which is fund-raising at the playground gate when the guy is completed!

Practical skills become important when a playground is faced with maintenance tasks such as mending electrical items or repairing a play structure. Their other main use is in teaching children how to use tools, or do basic repairs themselves.

Children of all abilities enjoy using tools, hammers and saws in particular, and some basic guidance needs to be given, to avoid injury and to ensure that they achieve the task they have set themselves, such as banging in a nail or sawing through a piece of wood. Similarly, mending or tinkering with bicycles and go-karts is a popular activity, but help needs to be on hand to show how chains can be reset without fingers getting caught, and punctures mended properly.

With children with disabilities, such advice may be doubly important. A child with a mental handicap, for instance, may need quite structured guidance and support when using a saw, and may have to be shown how to do it a number of times before she understands why it has to be used in such a way and becomes skilled in handling it appropriately. A good playworker recognises that any sign of impatience at having to repeat advice already given could be very disheartening for the child, and therefore takes care to give reminders in an encouraging way, helping the child towards an eventual justified sense of achievement.

It has to be remembered in this context that many children and adults with disabilities have, through over-protection and a lack of awareness of their potential abilities, been denied opportunities to acquire skills. The practical skills that a playworker can impart may help to reveal and develop new or hitherto dormant abilities.

One practical skill which needs separate mention is the ability to organise. An adventure playground needs a basic administrative system behind it if it is to operate effectively. This involves skills to do with money management, planning trips and holidays with children, organising volunteer and transport rotas, ensuring that there is regular contact between management and staff, keeping health and safety records up to date, working out a system of relaying messages from the telephone to the appropriate people, dealing with mail, ensuring that registers on children and general information are available, preparing for committee meetings, and, probably most important of all, making sure that there are enough staff on duty at any one time to open the playground for use by children. Such skills can certainly be learnt through experience, but if staff do not already possess them, they should be developed as rapidly as possible. It would be wrong for staff and management to think that an adventure playground, based on concepts of flexibility and freedom to pursue a variety of opportunities, can do without an administrative base.

If a project is to perform its function effectively, it cannot exist in isolation. It is important for playground staff to have skills in liaison and publicity. The project's work needs to be promoted through publications, meetings and individual face-to-face contact. Staff and management must therefore co-operate to convince as wide an audience as possible of the importance of their work.

Playstaff have a unique opportunity while actually on site to show parents, teachers, other professionals and potential donors of money or equipment what happens on a playground. Gaining the confidence of adults who have contact with children outside the playground is very important, so that when children arrive on site they are allowed to use the project in the way intended, without being held back from taking part in such activities as outdoor cooking or climbing structures. The more confidence parents and visiting staff have in the project and its workers, the easier it will be for children and adults to feel able to take part in adventure play. Public relations work helps to develop that confidence.

If possible, workers should visit the schools, hospitals, hostels and homes that use the playground; as well as being a good way to promote the scheme and gather confidence in it, this enables them to show an interest in the work of other people, and build a closer working relationship with the organisations that use the playground's facilities. It may also be necessary for staff to attend meetings, seminars or conferences and speak about the work of play projects which cater for children with disabilities.

Staff should also learn how to liaise with other agencies and individuals such as physiotherapists, medical staff and social workers, maintaining regular contact by telephone, letters and attendance at meetings, and sharing ideas about the playground's work. Other professionals should be aware of its importance, know what they can contribute to it and realise how playstaff may be able to contribute to their own work.

Essential knowledge

If playstaff are to make full use of their skills, these need to be combined with appropriate background knowledge. Workers on any play project should be familiar with the nature of the play process; on adventure playgrounds catering for children with disabilities, a thorough grounding in the concept of adventure play should be backed up by an understanding of the particular ways in which this relates to the children with whom they are dealing.

Play is an educational process which takes children through various stages of development, whether in a playgroup, at home or on an adventure playground. These stages are outlined in numerous publications on play, including Newson's *Toys and Playthings* and Arnold's *Your Child's Play*. Play staff should be aware of these stages of development; an understanding of them is particularly relevant to many children with disabilities.

If children have had limited play opportunities, or are developmentally impaired, as in the case of mental handicap, they may have missed some of these stages. When such children arrive on a play site they will want to regress to activities which they might normally be expected to have outgrown.

This happened in the case of one boy of fourteen who had spina bifida. He always arrived at the playground clean and well dressed and came from a background which encouraged this strongly. After several weeks on the project, where he managed to remain almost spotless, he gradually became more interested in the water play activities taking place in the pond. Suddenly one day he was found with his wheelchair half in the pond, splashing and shouting with the other children. He was then encouraged to wear wellington boots and old jeans and shirts, initially supplied by the playground, and to get more involved in playing with water and sand. In conversation with him it transpired that he had never been allowed to get wet or dirty and had always been in a position of watching others but not participating himself. His experience of water was limited to washing. He needed to experiment and play with, and in, the water, mix it with sand, gain new tactile feelings and, perhaps above all, get wet and dirty. His reactions to this when he really started to play were reminiscent of those of a much younger child, even a baby, splashing in a bath or paddling pool. The playground gave him the much-needed chance to pass through this stage of development, which he had previously missed out on.

Within the area of mental handicap, knowledge of the play process is useful in judging how and why certain play activities appeal to people with differing degrees of mental impairment. A severely mentally handicapped child with a developmental age of two, for instance, will indulge in play appropriate for that age, even though, in terms of chronological age and physical development, she may be twelve years old. It is important to realise this and plan opportunities which she can cope with, rather than attempt activities which are far too advanced and complex. To ignore a child's stage of development can cause confusion, frustration and anger for the child, whose needs will not be met.

Some children with mental handicaps simply do not know how to play. These are usually people who are severely impaired, and have perhaps been institutionalised for long periods. It then becomes the task of workers literally to teach these children how to play by, for instance, sitting in a sand pit with them and holding the child's hand, showing her how to manage a spade or bucket by physically guiding her movements. Such individuals will not play unless given this very structured support; this was the case with Robert, whom we mentioned earlier in this chapter. The process of getting such children motivated is often a long and frustrating one, but when a spontaneous reaction is gained, such as a football being kicked without encouragement, staff are likely to feel a sense of achievement and relief, which should be translated into praise and encouragement for the child.

We feel it is important to realise that some children do not know how to play, and also that some children feel inhibited in playing. Our experience has shown that there are a number of children with disabilities using play projects, who are like this and who do not indulge in spontaneous activities. Staff should know this and plan their work to take account of such children, who would otherwise get little benefit from using an adventure playground.

Knowledge of play needs to be allied to a knowledge of children and, with playgrounds which are used by children with disabilities, a knowledge of disability. The reference section of this book lists some useful publications dealing with children with disabilities, and other chapters look at some of the issues surrounding children with disabilities using play projects. In addition to this information, one current development needs to be recognised.

The field of disability is changing, albeit slowly. People with disabilities and their families are becoming more vocal, and in some cases angry, about the way they have been, and continue to be, treated. They are at last finding a voice with which to press for their rights and to confront able-bodied society with the issues that surround disability, particularly the issue of people's attitudes; we refer readers to Allan Sutherland's *Disabled We Stand* for a fuller discussion of this. This shift in response, whereby a traditionally passive group are now speaking up, should be recognised by those who are involved in play provision with children with disabilities.

Adventure playgrounds are places where people are helped to grow, develop and learn through a variety of play experiences. Much of this is achieved through the opportunity for self-expression and contact with others. This should in turn lead to an increase in confidence and skills which will enable children with disabilities to become stronger and more assertive in the years ahead when they will often have to battle against the many prejudices and barriers that are placed in their way. This may sound like a somewhat idealised vision of what a playground can offer, but we genuinely believe that these projects have the potential to offer children this kind of support and confidence, which will serve them well in later life. We should like to see adventure playgrounds, and indeed other forms of play provision that cater for children with disabilities, ally themselves with the movement towards greater self-expression among, and recognition of the rights of, people with disabilities. It is something that we feel able-bodied workers have an increasing responsibility to consider and act upon.

A knowledge of health and safety procedures is essential for all playworkers. Every project should draw up its own health and safety policy document and all staff abide by it. Such varied concerns as animal care, safety of fencing, maintenance of heating systems and an adequate first aid kit are all part of any health and safety programme. We strongly recommend that the NPFA's *Towards a Safer Adventure Playground*, a comprehensive document whose contents should be familiar to all staff, be used as a model from which projects can draw up their own policies.

Many people have felt that health and safety regulations have taken much of the spontaneity and vigour out of adventure play. This may be true insofar as workers may have to think twice about certain activities, such as letting children build a tree house or dig a tunnel. But there is no excuse for exposing children to real danger, such as the possibility of a tunnel collapsing because it has not been properly shored up. 'Spontaneity' should not be made an excuse for gross irresponsibility. Health and safety guidelines, ultimately backed up by the law, have eliminated a lot of sloppy mistakes and made staff think harder about how to develop a play environment where children can play adventurously without being exposed to serious risk.

There is, of course, a danger of carrying safety rules to such an extreme that a playground becomes sterile and boring. This is as bad as a project which ignores guidelines completely. Staff must balance the need for adventure and excitement with the requirements for a safe environment. The two are not necessarily contradictory, but do need some thought and discussion by the workers and management concerned.

A familiarity with surrounding statutory and voluntary services is important for all staff. A knowledge of outside agencies and what they do is highly relevant to a project's work. Staff should be aware, for example, of how the Community or District Mental Handicap Team could provide valuable advice and assistance, particularly in terms of referring children to the playground, or how a local PHAB or MENCAP group could help with transport or share in organising a fair or concert to raise money.

An understanding of the policy issues that surround many of these bodies is also useful, because this will help a playground put its work in perspective in terms of social policy. The immediate example that comes to mind here is the publication in 1978 of the Warnock Report and the subsequent passing of the 1981 Education Act. Both of these documents signified a change of direction within the educational system towards a more integrated approach in schooling. They also recommended increased rights for parents in the process of choosing where, and how, their child should be educated, a recognition of the increasing say being demanded by people with disabilities and their families. Playgrounds should be aware of this change and the impact it is going to have on the special school system, for there is no doubt in our minds that adventure play projects will be affected sooner or later by the impact of such pieces of legislation, just as they have been by the Health and Safety at Work Act.

It is helpful, too, to have some knowledge of existing play services, both statutory and voluntary. Play projects often come together under an umbrella Play Association or Play Council, which can facilitate discussion, support and training: participation in these bodies should always be encouraged. A knowledge of national play organisations, such as the recently-created PLAYBOARD, can provide access to information and resources or the opportunity to bring people together from different parts of the country to discuss their work, as happens with the National Standing Conference.

We would also remind readers that many children who use play projects are not white and come from different ethnic backgrounds. It is therefore important that staff are aware and informed about the varying needs of different groups of children. Thus, when preparing and cooking food for a barbecue, staff should realise that a Hindu child will not eat pork sausages or any food that is cooked in lard (pork fat). It would be insensitive to go ahead with this activity when a Hindu child is using the playground, without taking account of these factors.

It is all too easy for white workers to organise and encourage activities based on their own cultural assumptions and forget that they are often working with children whose language, religion, family structure, diet and recreational tastes are sometimes dramatically different from their own or those of white children. Just as staff need to become informed about disability, so they need to learn about the issues raised by life in a multi-racial society. We recommend that readers refer to Fair Play for Children's publication *All Children Play* for advice and help.

Training

All playstaff should have access to training opportunities. Given all that has been discussed in this chapter, it is obvious that there are many skills to be developed, and much knowledge to be acquired, if a worker is to perform his job effectively. Even experienced staff need to have their skills and knowledge regularly reappraised. The purpose of training is not simply to teach new skills and pass on new knowledge, but also to enable workers to stand back and consider the work that a playground is doing. Getting away from the day-to-day pressure should enable staff to take a more distanced, possibly more rational, view of what they are doing. This helps to put their work in perspective, so that they can examine it objectively both in its own right and in relation to other agencies and services. It should also help to break the isolation that many playworkers feel when on their projects.

Such opportunities usually take the form of what is often termed 'in-service' training, being done on a part-time basis. This kind of training can be arranged by existing play organisations; the London Adventure Playground Association (LAPA), for example, organises part-time courses for playstaff on subjects ranging from structure building to working with girls. As far as disability is concerned, numerous bodies run courses, conferences and seminars on a whole range of issues.

The Spastics Society runs year-round training events at its Castle Priory College near Oxford for both new and experienced staff who work with people with disabilities in all kinds of settings. MENCAP, PHAB and NAWCH are three others who run courses and conferences at both local and national levels. To find out about such opportunities, projects should contact the relevant organisations and ask to be put on their mailing lists for newsletters and circulars.

Visits to schools, hospitals and residential homes can also be seen as training opportunities. Such facilities often welcome visitors who want to spend a day or longer in the classroom or hospital ward finding out at first hand what goes on there. Inviting people who work in these places, such as speech therapists, to talk to playworkers in a neutral setting is another way of picking up new skills and knowledge.

Full-time training courses for adventure playground workers are virtually non-existent at present. The only full-time college-based course in the United Kingdom is the one-year course offered by Thurrock Technical College in Essex, leading to its Diploma in Playleadership. LAPA runs a one-year traineeship course for a small number of new workers. This involves work on a playground, interspersed with regular weekly training sessions. Other play organisations are attempting similar programmes. But all of them are working on limited finances, and the struggle to establish comprehensive training opportunities, whether part- or full-time, will continue for some while yet. Playgrounds who want advice on how and where training can be implemented should contact the Joint National Committee on Training for Playleadership, a body which is trying to bring together the existing training programmes and gain greater recognition, from statutory authorities in particular, for play training programmes.

These are only brief comments on what is a crucial area for the effective development of playwork; we urge staff and management to take whatever opportunities they can to participate in, and organise, training events. Adventure play will stagnate if those who are meant to be facilitating it ignore, or miss, the opportunity to develop their own skills and abilities.

Playwork is a demanding, yet fascinating, job. If it is to be adequately done, it requires a wide range of skills and knowledge, equivalent to those that are necessary to be a successful teacher or community worker, even though the status that its workers are accorded by many employing authorities, and other professionals, does not compare with that given to teaching staff or community workers. One major reason for such attitudes is that many people are not aware of the kind of work that playgrounds do, and the skills involved are not necessarily obviously apparent; the sight of a child such as Robert descending a slide gives an outsider little indication of the many weeks of work, and numerous hours of planning, that have made that apparently simple action possible.

5   Day-to-day Experiences

The purpose of this chapter is to give the reader a view of what goes on during one day at an adventure playground for handicapped children. It will bring together points made in other parts of this book and attempt to provide a picture of activities that take place and issues that arise during any one day. The way in which events are described is not necessarily the only 'right' way to attempt them: different methods may work equally well – indeed, an important part of the adventure play philosophy is to experiment with different ideas and methods as much as possible. All of the areas covered in this chapter are based on first hand experience.

Most playgrounds open their doors at 9–9.30 am. during both school termtime and holiday periods. Whatever the opening time, it is very important that the full-time staff always arrive at work on time. Good timekeeping is part of the contract of employment, but is also part of the informal contract that workers should have with the users of the project. Consistently poor timekeeping can lose staff the respect, not only of the children and adults who use the scheme, but also of parents, volunteers and management members. It is also most annoying for staff who are always prompt and who will already be working on preparing the site for the day's work when latecomers arrive.

The first task of playworkers when they arrive is to check the playground for any damage or vandalism that may have occurred overnight. This means looking over the building and outdoor area and making sure that fencing, windows, structures, gates and the like are ready and safe for children. Break-ins to buildings are not an uncommon event on most projects, and can provide a depressing start to the day. If the break-in is serious it should be reported to the police immediately (although they may already have been informed by neighbours, or by the ringing of an alarm bell). Remember that insurance companies will expect projects to have reported break-ins to the police before they will meet a claim. If windows are broken they need to be repaired as quickly as possible; in particular, the broken glass must be cleared up or taken out of the frame straight away. It is not unknown for fires to have been started underneath play structures or big fences, so be aware of this possibility. Damaged fencing, caused by people trying to climb it or attacking it with hammers or other tools, is also quite frequent and needs to be checked for. Most handicapped adventure playgrounds have sand pits, and it is important that they are checked every morning before use, and if possible raked over. In hot weather, it can also be useful to water the sand to keep it damp enough for castle-building.

It is useful to develop a list – mental or written – of all the areas that need to be checked before children arrive so that the site is safe from obvious hazards and ready for them to use. Where repairs are necessary, put them in hand straight away. When there is only time to make a temporary repair until later in the day, that is good enough so long as the damage is made safe or secure. If it can not be fully repaired, always record such damage in an incident book so that if accidents occur later you have at least noted the problem and started to put its full repair into operation. This could be important if a claim for damages were to be made against the playground. (This is a precaution to cover staff against remote possibilities; if it seems genuinely likely that an accident could be caused, that part of the site, or the playground as a whole, should be closed until repairs are carried out rather than put the children at risk; failure to do so would be a breach of a playground's moral responsibilities if not a criminal offence.)

Once the site has been checked it needs to be prepared for use. This entails getting out mobile equipment and ensuring it is suitable for use – the wheels are not about to fall off! – putting out sand and water play equipment, mixing up paints for use in the craft area, putting up the ropes (which should have been stored indoors overnight to prevent vandalism), checking cloakrooms and lavatories and making sure that there are adequate supplies available of such items as orange juice, toilet rolls, soap and towels to see the playground through the day.

The combination of checking the site and preparing it for use, particularly if there are repairs to be made, can take a little while and perhaps immediately illustrates how difficult it is to run a playground with just one or two staff. On a project with four staff these duties can be split between them and less time taken, but with fewer staff there will be greater pressure and less time.

We should like to emphasise the importance of getting a playground ready by the time the children arrive. This is based on two principles. One is the health and safety aspect of the project: a playground must be safe for children to use. The second is that children must feel the project is welcoming them and that there are many opportunities open to them when they arrive. If the project is prepared, has equipment and staff ready, children and visiting adults will respond positively and make the best use of the playground. A badly organised scheme will not be ready to accept children and the users will respond accordingly through disruptive behaviour and petty vandalism.

At the beginning of the day it may also be necessary to do some administrative work. This can be extremely difficult when children are around as they invariably demand one's attention, which it is difficult to give when on the phone or writing letters, so it is preferable to do it before they arrive. Other times to carry out this work may be at lunch time or at the end of the day. It is useful to tell people to ring at times when you know children will not be around, or when there will not be too many, for there is nothing more frustrating than being called to the phone while helping a child up a ladder or supervising a barbecue fire.

When children arrive they should be welcomed. This, as we have stated above, is partly done by having the site ready, but is also achieved by staff actively welcoming children and accompanying adults. This immediately provides a warm and friendly atmosphere from which to launch activities. We have visited playgrounds of all descriptions where long faces greet everyone. While this is understandable in the middle of a cold winter's day or after a bad break-in, a depressed, almost hostile atmosphere will be transmitted to the children very quickly, and will affect what goes on during the day. It is also important at the end of a day, or of a session, to say goodbye to children and adults. Just as a good welcome makes children feel at home, so a happy departure makes them feel their presence has been worthwhile and valued (even if they have been the bane of a worker's day!).

When children are on site, they are able to take part in a variety of activities. Of these, barbecues are probably one of the most popular: few playgrounds will get through a day without having one or having staff being pursued by children who want one. We should like to make some points in relation to this activity which are important in the context of adventure play.

Most children with disabilities will come across fire only in limited ways, perhaps through the cooker at home or school, through seeing people use matches, or through coal fires. Their understanding of it may therefore be limited and naive. What a playground can do is provide substance and meaning to the flames and heat that emanate from a fire. Therefore, if a child or group of children wants to cook pancakes on an outside fire it is important that the fire is not blazing away, with the pancake mixture prepared. The process of creating the fire needs to be gone through. Paper has to be found, wood collected, the fire built and then started. If the wood is wet or too large it will not catch light, and will need to be changed for smaller pieces. Having the fire in a contained area such as a brick barbecue or half an oil drum, attached to a supporting frame, is important so that children realise that fire has to be easily controlled and not allowed to get out of hand.

Once the fire is going, the next problem is how to keep it alight, part of which consists in discovering what *not* to put on a fire – foam rubber and plastics, for instance. When the fire is no longer needed it should be put out; involving children in this part of the process is also important.

Through barbecues children can learn what fire is and how it can be used. They will encounter the dangers involved but also the pleasures, such as warmth on a cold day and the cooking of food. If they are deprived of this experience they will never understand or learn to cope with fire, which could, in later years, lead to accidents or mistakes that could prove very harmful.

Similarly, if food is to be cooked on an open fire it should be prepared by the children, not be ready and waiting. For pancakes this means mixing ingredients and preparing utensils and frying pans. A great sense of satisfaction and fun can be gained from the process of preparing food, making a fire, cooking and ultimately eating the food, and a very positive learning experience enjoyed. We know of many outdoor gourmets of all disabilities, whom adults were most wary of letting near open fires, but who proved themselves able and skilful. The adage on which many playgrounds operate, of 'give children the opportunity and they will rise to it', has proved itself many times over with this activity.

It is essential that any fire must be supervised by a member of the playground staff, or another responsible adult. No child, able-bodied or disabled, should be left on his own in an adventure playground with an open fire. It is useful to have a barbecue fire raised above ground level. This enables children in wheelchairs to use the fire for cooking much more easily, as they do not have to bend down to ground level, and it also provides a better balanced position for everyone else to use the fire, particularly if they are holding frying pans or pots. Also, if a fire is raised off ground level it can not spread, being in a contained area. It makes using grills easier, too.

Mobile equipment is in use every day. Most projects have bicycles or go-karts that have been adapted for use by physically disabled children, and these should only be used by this group, or the constant wear and tear will simply halve their usable life. Besides, these will be the most expensive pieces of mobile equipment that a playground possesses and a project will simply not be able to afford to keep replacing them. The other equipment in use will range from bought trolleys and scooters to second-hand bikes that would otherwise be thrown out by families, and home-made go-karts. No matter how battered some of these vehicles may look, children will try to use them until the equipment literally gives way beneath them. This means that a daily task for workers and children, is the patching up of these items until they can be patched up no more!

It is important when mobile equipment is being used to make sure that it is not interfering with other playground activities and is not creating hazards for other children. For instance, pathways are the obvious avenue for bicycles to be ridden on but other children may be walking or sitting near a path and their needs must be considered too. Riding a vehicle or pulling a trolley up a ramp or down a slide may also be dangerous and needs to be watched for. Children do get excited when riding go-karts and bikes and at times this excitement can overspill. Playground staff need to be on hand to deal with this when it occurs.

A common problem on playgrounds is that there are not enough of the popular vehicles to go round all the children who want to use them. Some go-karts are used more than others and children will argue and fight over who should have them. This is an example of a situation where staff can help to make sure that everyone gets a fair use of equipment and thus defuse potentially disruptive situations. A solution employed on some projects is to have a list upon which children place their names. Each child has 10–15 minutes and knows he or she has to hand the bike on to the next person on the list after that time. If they want another go they place their name back on the list. If this system is operated with the consent and agreement of the children it often proves most successful.

It is sensible not to have too many pieces of mobile equipment, for several reasons. If the playground site is small, a constant stream of bicycles, go-karts and trolleys whizzing around can be disruptive. Constantly maintaining those pieces of equipment can take up time as well, time perhaps better spent on other activities. Finally, the amount of storage space taken up by vehicles may preclude other items, such as inflatables, from being properly stored, which will increase the time that has to be spent on their maintenance and repair.

Another area of daily activity on playgrounds revolves around the care of animals. Rabbits, guinea pigs, mice, fish, birds, even donkeys and snakes, have all been kept on playgrounds, and invariably all catch the imagination and concern of children using the projects. Two points need to be made straight away in relation to animals. First, a playground must be satisfied that it can properly house, feed and look after any animals it possesses. Well-built hutches and runs, ample feed supplies and time to clean cages and fish tanks are essential elements to bear in mind when planning to have animals. It is unfair and cruel to have creatures that can not be properly cared for. From our personal experience it is always novel and interesting to get a new animal and persuade ourselves that the project can look after it. But after a while the novelty can wear off, and in consequence the animal may not be looked after as well as it should be.

Secondly, there is a danger of a playground having so many pets that too much time is taken up looking after them and other activities are ignored. Costs, such as veterinary fees, could also escalate, which could create problems for projects working on limited budgets.

It is important that children take part in the feeding and cleaning of the playground pets, so that they realise that if the animals are to survive and thrive they need care and protection. Holding and stroking creatures is an interesting tactile experience for children, particularly when the animals respond to the person holding them by moving or making a noise. For many children with disabilities, first-hand contact with animals is limited, and a playground can make up for this lack of experience by bringing children face to face with them. In this respect it is interesting to note the success of Riding for the Disabled, and how well disabled children have responded to this activity. We would recommend that projects also try to find out if there are any local farms that can be visited so that children can come into contact with larger animals such as cows and horses. In rural areas there are often farmers who welcome visits by groups of children. In town or city areas we recommend that the City Farms Advisory Service (address in reference section) be contacted, for possible visits to existing city farms, and advice on the care of animals.

A final point in relation to day-to-day care of pets: when a playground closes they must be securely locked away so that they are not stolen or attacked. Animals have been killed or maimed on several occasions as a result of not being safely locked in their cages, or of being placed in cages which were easily vandalised. Animals should be locked inside the play building, or in a secure shed such as the former railway carriage used at Fulham Palace playground.

The structures and swings on a playground obviously get intensive day-to-day use. They therefore need to be strongly and properly built, and regularly checked for any faults or damage. Different children will use structures in different ways and should be given the opportunity to do so. Thus, a climbing tower with several platforms can be used as a fort by one group of children and made into a house with tables and chairs by another. Other children will use it as a climbing structure alone and not consider it in any other way. This again illustrates the flexibility that should be built into an adventure play project, with which workers need to feel comfortable.

As discussed in the chapter on equipment, access is one of the key considerations when designing play structures. Ramps, ladders and stairs to varying heights and angles should provide different ways of getting on to and off equipment and once on a structure movement around it needs to be relatively easy. It is perhaps on climbing frames, slides, swings and platforms that the question of 'how far can we allow the children to use them on their own?' arises. Children with little or no eyesight, children with problems of balance and mobility, mentally handicapped children who appear fearless – all daily pose difficult questions to staff while the playground structures are in use. When should workers stand back and let the children attempt things on their own? When is a little coaxing, physical or verbal, necessary? These questions have to be answered on the spot and depend on the workers' knowledge of the children using the project. What we would say, though, is that these children are on an adventure playground, where they must experience challenge and excitement, and decisions on intervention should take this into account. Two examples may help to illustrate several of these points.

A spina-bifida child in a wheelchair became bored one day with going up a structure via a ramp and decided to use the stairs that everyone else used. He took his wheelchair up to the base of the stairs, pulled himself out of it and proceeded to go up the steps backwards, on his bottom. He never used the ramp again, but regularly climbed the stairs in this way from then on – just as legitimate a way of using stairs as the conventional one, we think.

The second example is that of a six-year-old Down's Syndrome child who managed to climb on to the top of a four inch beam, eight feet above ground, which supported a single track rail swing which travelled some thirty yards. The child – to the horror of playground staff – proceeded to walk along this beam with great speed and enthusiasm. Thinking that making a fuss would distract the child, staff stood and held their breath. He walked the length of the beam, climbed happily down, smiled at petrified staff and walked off. Interestingly, he never did it again!

Play also takes place within the building. One of the most popular pastimes is use of the craft area, where paint, clay, wood and many other materials are available for children to experiment with. Mobiles which can hang from ceilings, paintings, puppets, masks can all be created in this activity. It is here that scrap material such as paper, yoghurt cartons, wool and cotton reels really come into their own. It is important to let children thoroughly explore the possibilities of such activities – let them, for instance, paint windows, walls and play structures as well as the more traditional paper on the table. Remember that many children with disabilities using adventure play-grounds have had limited opportunities to play with these materials, and need experience of doing so.

Dressing up clothes are another popular stimulus for indoor play activities. They encourage fantasy play, and often provide endless hours of fun and enjoyment for children. On one playground where a set of old army uniforms and a wedding costume had been been recently donated, the royal wedding ceremony was re-enacted by the children. This activity took up the whole of one afternoon and involved everyone, adults included, in dressing up and taking a part.

As a day progresses, running repairs and maintenance always become necessary. Lights fuse, drains get blocked, equipment breaks, a window may get smashed; all will need to be dealt with quickly. A day on a playground will not go by without an incident of this sort. Hence the need to have tools and resources to hand so that repairs can be swiftly carried out.

Not all maintenance and repairs can be carried out quickly on the spot; some jobs will take a day or more to complete. It is therefore a good idea to close the playground for maintenance days or for a regular maintenance week. A good time to do this would be after a major holiday programme, when the site will have undergone great wear and tear from constant use. A number of projects do already operate this way of working and there is no doubt that it enables them to get through a great deal of maintenance and repair work which in the long run benefits the users of the playgrounds.

Children, too, often need patching up, and again it is rare for a day to go by without a child falling over or having some other minor accident. Every playground should have at least two of its staff, and preferably all, qualified in first aid. (The Red Cross or St John Ambulance should be contacted for advice about training courses.) Besides having trained staff, each project should have a good first aid kit that is readily available when an accident happens. This kit must be regularly checked, as it will quickly run out of some items and if staff are not careful an incident will occur for which they have no, or little, first aid material. The playground should also possess an accident book in which all accidents are recorded. This is necessary under health and safety regulations and is common practice in all workplaces.

For staff in handicapped adventure playgrounds first aid awareness is doubly important. If, for example, a hydrocephalic child bangs her head heavily in a fall, it will be necessary to take that child to hospital for a check-up to see if any damage has been done, particularly to the inserted valve. If a child has an epileptic fit, or appears to be going into one, staff must be aware of how to handle it, and if a brittle-boned child gets badly bruised staff must know how to deal with it. Most importantly, playworkers need to know which children are on drugs, how often they are taken and in what combinations, and what effect the drugs have on them, such as making them sleepy or unco-ordinated in their actions or speech.

It is always valuable to get information on the above points from visiting parents or school staff. If it helps, record this information on paper so that you know exactly what the problem is and how it is usually treated. When medication needs to be taken during the day, make sure it is kept safely until it is needed. This awareness is also useful for playworkers on other play projects who are attempting to integrate children with disabilities on to their sites.

A day on an adventure playground for handicapped children will bring staff into contact with children of varying needs and disabilities. This can prove to be a challenging, and tiring, experience. Multiply-handicapped children, for instance, will need almost constant one-to-one attention if they are to benefit from a visit to a playground. They will need to be physically pushed, and possibly carried, if they want to use equipment. It may take time to find an activity that they enjoy, and when it is found their attention span may be such that the activity is only interesting for a few minutes. (Further information and advice on adventure play and the severely handicapped may be found in the chapter on play in a residential setting.)

Communication with such children may also be difficult. A worker's range of verbal skills will be tested to the limit, and other forms of communication, such as touching, hand or arm movements and facial expressions may be necessary. With many mentally handicapped children it may be useful for staff to have a basic knowledge of the Makaton vocabulary of signs which is taught in schools.

Working with extremely active autistic children can present a different picture. These children often have bizarre and repetitive behaviour patterns, which reach obsessional levels, and also display a seeming shyness and unwillingness to communicate with anybody, whether staff or other children. Establishing a relationship with these children can take a great deal of time and requires patience and tact. Once it is established some positive work can be done.

Danny is an autistic boy who has used an adventure playground for several years now. At first he was obsessed with water play. He used two receptacles, which had to be the same ones each day, to pour water in and out of unceasingly. He did this standing by an outdoor stream which led to the playground pond. If his activity was disrupted, he became upset and disturbed. Gradually, over a period of months, it became possible to change receptacles, add soap bubbles to the water and also coloured dyes, so that variety and interest was added to his play and it became less obsessional. Eventually, over a period of several years, Danny was weaned off his obsession with water play and was able to join in other playground activities of which he had previously been shy or frightened.

Working with deaf children gives yet another perspective, and another communication challenge; thinking about how blind or partially sighted children might best use a playground provides yet more food for thought and discussion. It is always very beneficial in these circumstances to talk to visiting school staff and parents, who will always provide information and advice on their children. The children themselves should of course be consulted as well, to find out how they like people to communicate and work with them, and what they see as their strengths and weaknesses in a playground setting. Having a disability does not make children unable to communicate their needs, desires, frustrations and angers to able-bodied workers or able-bodied children. Indeed, it is important for staff to encourage such expression at every level.

Adjusting to children's different intellectual levels is also a challenge. Many disabled youngsters have clear language and a clear understanding of concepts and can be communicated with very adequately. But with some mentally handicapped children different issues have to be faced. A child may need to be told something, or shown how to go about some activity, many times over. The outdoor fire described earlier in this chapter is a good example of an event which may have to be repeated again and again before some children fully grasp how to do it and the ideas behind it. Often, logical thought processes become confused and strained, which can cause children to become upset and angry. This needs to be borne in mind when disciplining such children.

Adjusting to the different levels of communicating and working with children with disabilities is not necessarily an easy process. Staff must be aware, though, that they need to consider this if they are to provide an effective service, and not miss or ignore the needs of the children they serve.

Playgrounds have a constant stream of visitors dropping in every day. These people can range from interested professionals or students on training courses wishing to find out more about this type of play provision, to local people dropping scrap materials in to the project or just coming in for a coffee and chat with staff and children. An adventure playground encourages this 'drop-in' kind of approach because of its seeming informality and the way in which this makes people feel relaxed and comfortable while on site. The community-based nature of these schemes also attracts local people in. We feel that this type of contact is most valuable for playgrounds and should be encouraged, although we would warn against having too many adults on site, bearing in mind that these are essentially child-oriented projects.

It is a particularly good idea to spend time talking to parents who bring their children down to use the playground. Not only do staff get a clearer picture about the children themselves, but they can also provide an 'ear' to a parent who might be feeling low and vulnerable and who needs someone to talk to. An adventure playground may also reveal information about children which has not been picked up before at home or at school, such as new skills in communication or increased mobility. Such information needs to be passed on to parents and other workers who have contact with the child, which can be done when these people visit the playground. Good communication with the adults who bring children down to the scheme, whether they be parents, teachers, nurses, brothers or sisters, pays good dividends in the long run, the greatest being a trust and respect for the playground and its staff which allows workers in turn to do very positive and exciting work with the children.

As the day draws to a close and children start to leave, the site has to be cleared up and secured. Essentially the reverse of what happens in the morning takes place. Equipment needs to be stored, rope swings dismantled, fires put out, sand pit and pond cleared, rubbish collected, animals housed in their night-time cages, urgent repairs seen to, and the building cleaned. This can take some time, but it is important that a site is cleared and made safe, ready, as far as possible, for the next day. It is certainly the experience of playgrounds where inappropriate tidying up and maintenance has taken place that it becomes much more difficult the next day to get a site ready for use, and it is also likely that theft or vandalism will have occurred overnight, particularly if security procedures have not been put into operation on closing.

On leaving the playground, it is important to ensure that all the kids have gone and that no one is left on site. Invariably, local children will get on to the playground after staff have gone; this really can not be stopped, but at least staff should, if an accident occurs, be covered by the project's insurance policy if they have made sure the site is clear when they leave it. In relation to this, a disclaimer notice needs to be placed at the playground entrance.

It is relevant in this review of day-to-day experiences to point out that off-site activities are a common feature of playground programmes. Day trips to other projects, fairs and places of interest all provide a change for children. Weekend or holiday camping trips also provide excitement and challenge which should be seen as part of the adventure concept. Such activities do require careful planning and thought: for instance, parental consent must be gained before children are taken off site and sensible budgeting has to be carried out, but there is no doubt in our minds that these events do add a different and useful dimension to a playground's work.

Every day on an adventure playground is different, and

presents its own challenge to staff and children. It is right that this is the case and that much of the day should be unpredictable and spontaneous in content. An adventure playground would not be an adventure playground if each day were the same. Staff must provide a base of administrative activity and correct health and safety procedure; from there it is up to users and workers to take the project where they will.

6 Resources

Materials

Adventure playgrounds used to be known as 'junk playgrounds', and the adventure playground movement has a long tradition of recycling waste materials, from old telegraph poles down to empty yoghurt cartons. This has often been due to sheer necessity: playgrounds tend to run on limited budgets, and to be forced to rely on 'scrounged' materials. But whatever level of finance is available, this way of doing things is worth sticking to, and should be seen as a positive benefit rather than an inferior substitute for doing things 'properly'.

In the first place, no playground has unlimited funds. There is little point in spending hundreds of pounds on commercially manufactured climbing frames when structures that are more fun, more attractive and just as safe can be constructed for a tenth of the cost. The money would be better spent on, for example, taking a group of kids on a camping holiday. And, while the bureaucrats responsible for the sterility of traditional playgrounds may find it simpler to fill in an order form and write a cheque, any adventure playground where money is in greater supply than labour and imagination is in deep trouble.

Even more importantly, waste materials give children greater freedom. We should not forget that children spend a lot of their lives – at school, at home and elsewhere – in adult-dominated surroundings where they learn that there are definite limits to the way they use what is around them. Tables are for sitting at, not for overturning to make a fort or a pirate ship. Water is for drinking or washing in, not for playing with. The more an adventure playground feels like a different sort of place, the easier it is for children to believe that it really is somewhere where most of these restrictions do not apply, where they are free to experiment, to make a mess and to let their imaginations run riot. Waste materials play an important part in creating that different atmosphere, by making a playground's actual physical appearance different from that of school or home.

This appearance reflects a very real difference. Because junk has little financial value, no one needs to worry about it getting damaged – whereas it would be a strong-minded playworker who encouraged the curiosity of a child who was engrossed in dismantling beyond repair a costly piece of commercially manufactured equipment. That freedom for experimentation allows children to become creators rather than passive consumers.

Scrounging for materials should be the joint responsibility of playworkers and playground management; quite how this responsibility is divided will vary from project to project, but it should never be forgotten that it is the playworkers who know best what the playground needs. They are the ones who are in daily contact with the children using the playground.

For best results, you should aim to get your local community as involved as possible in keeping the playground supplied with materials. Let people know what the playground is doing, and what it needs. Put out a newsletter, organise an exhibition of photographs in a local library, check whether your local council produces any publications that might carry news about your activities and needs. Use your local media, particularly if anything newsworthy happens: though a news story may not produce direct results, it helps remind people of your playground's existence, so that they'll be more willing to help if you approach them personally. Thus, when a lorry-load of building waste was illegally dumped on Charlie Chaplin playground, the South London Press carried both a photograph and a sob-story about how money raised for handicapped children would have to be used to clear it. (If you are unsure about how to approach the press, get hold of Denis MacShane's *Using the Media*.)

Your eventual aim should be to build up a network of support throughout your local community. Start with the people who already have some involvement with the playground, such as parents and teachers of children who use it. You will find that many people who might be uncomfortable with a more formal involvement, such as joining your management committee, will be happy to help in other ways, such as donating cast-off clothes for children to change into when they get wet or muddy, or helping paint play structures. Then try to build contacts with the people who live around the playground. Even if you don't know them, they will certainly have noticed you, and be curious about what you're doing – so why not hold an Open Day and let them see for themselves? Find out if there's a local Tenants' Association you could work through.

Approach local schools – not simply the special schools that may use the playground. They may well like the idea of encouraging their pupils to support your project by, for example, organising a collection of old toys and games. Their pupils may also provide a useful source of performers if you're running a special event. They may even be prepared to use their woodwork and metalwork shops to make items of equipment for the playground.

And approach people individually. If you keep animals, see if there's a local greengrocer who'd be prepared to save his waste greens to feed them. Find out if there's a local councillor who takes a particular interest in disability – or try to *get* one interested – and who can advise you on the various forms of assistance that may be available from your local authority. You should aim to have contact with every level of local society: at Chelsea playground, a local dosser used to come in every Monday morning and clear up the playground in return for his breakfast – a profitable arrangement for both sides!

Above all, remember that your aim is to get people *involved* with the playground. When they do help you, make them feel appreciated. Write letters of thanks where appropriate, or thank people personally, show them round the playground if they haven't seen it, keep them in touch with how things are going. (This is one way in which a newsletter can come in useful.) The more that local people care about the playground, and feel that *they* are helping it to succeed, the more they will continue to support it regularly.

One thing that all adventure playgrounds need to scrounge for is building materials, particularly heavy timber for building play structures. The basis of most structures is old telegraph poles. These are cheap and easy to get hold of: most telephone works depots are happy to sell off 'dead' poles at a minimal price. Demolition contractors provide a useful source of joists and floorboards. It's worth trying to build a regular relationship with one or more local firms, because timber is something you will always need. So don't forget to give the people working on the demolition site something to buy themselves a drink with. (But bear in mind that the line between grateful appreciation and illegality is a fine one: you may get offered certain 'favours' that it would be sensible to refuse.)

Develop also the habit of keeping an eye on builders' skips: the rubble that they contain may include perfectly usable materials such as timber, and old bricks that can be recycled. And, as always, make sure that as many people as possible know what you need: when Charlie Chaplin playground was opening, we obtained a lot of wood as a result of an appeal broadcast by a local radio station. There is, however, one type of wood which is very easy to get hold of – and which you are almost certain to be offered if you put out a widespread appeal – which you should be very wary of: old fork-lift pallets. Many factories are delighted to get rid of these, and will even deliver them by the lorry-load, but they are made from very poor quality wood, good for little but burning (and even then, it's hardly worth the amount of work it takes to break them up!)

Avoid, or get rid of, wood that is badly splintered or cracked, and therefore liable to be dangerous for children to handle. If you use wood regularly for barbecues, it is useful to maintain a supply that has been cut up and stored ready for use.

Equally easy to obtain, but a good deal more useful than pallets, are old tyres. You should be able to get these free from almost any garage or car-breaker's yard. But, precisely because they are so easy to get hold of when you need them, don't build up large stores of them: piles of tyres burn easily, with an unpleasant black smoke, and make an attractive target for vandalism.

One of the biggest problems with scrounging building materials is transport: though you may sometimes persuade people to deliver them (especially with demolition firms, where you may be saving them the cost of transporting the wood to somewhere farther away), a lot will be available to you only on condition that you can pick them up, which means that you have got to get hold of a lorry. If you are in a city large enough to have an Adventure Playground or Play Association, they may own one. If not, try local organisations, such as the Territorial Army. Perhaps a local firm might be prepared to donate the use of a lorry and driver for a day from time to time. Does your local Rotary Club have any suitable contacts? Might your local council be able to help? What do other local adventure playgrounds do? If you are putting out a large-scale appeal, such as on the radio, make sure you've got this problem solved *before* the appeal goes out.

You should also consider the possibility of organising joint appeals with other local projects. This is particularly likely to be valuable if you are having problems with transport: another project may have its own contacts, or may be willing to split hire costs.

Building materials, especially if they come from a demolition site, should always be checked for potential danger. Remove any nails that are sticking out of your wood, remove any wiring and other metal fixtures left on telegraph posts. Check the condition of tyres, particularly those that are reinforced with steel, which can splinter, leaving sharp bits of metal sticking out: get rid of any that are dangerously worn. Keep a look-out for toxic waste (such as the asbestos rabbit-hutch that was donated to one playground we know); if you find any, contact your local Environmental Health Inspector, who should be able to arrange for safe disposal. If you are storing materials on the playground, do all this when they arrive; don't wait until you're about to use them.

A playground also needs a constant supply of toys, and you should be able to obtain most of these free or very cheaply. Teachers and parents who use the playground will probably be willing to donate toys that their children have grown out of. As suggested earlier, local schools and other organisations may be willing to organise an appeal. Local shops may be willing to donate new toys. Use jumble sales and charity shops; if you explain your needs to them, you may find that charity shops will be willing to put some items aside for you when they are donated to them. Jumble sales are particularly valuable as a source of dressing-up clothes; if you hang around to the end of a large jumble sale, you may find that they will be willing to give you unsold items, or let you have a load of clothes at a knockdown price.

Find out whether you have a Toy Library in your area: ask other play organisations or write directly to PLAY MATTERS. This association's *Good Toy Guide* contains a section on 'toys for people with special needs' which, even if you can't afford to buy new toys, might give you ideas you can adapt for toys you can make, or persuade someone else to make for you. And never forget that your definition of 'toys' should be much wider than that of a commercial toy company, covering anything that children will enjoy playing with, whether or not it was originally manufactured as a toy. Kids can, for example, have a lot of fun with an old telephone – or, better still, two old telephones, so that two children can hold a conversation 'over the phone'. Old cash registers are also great fun.

As with other donated materials, always check toys to see whether they are in usable condition, and whether they present any potential dangers. Toys may have been cast off because they are broken, leaving sharp edges which could cut a child. Be particularly careful with electrical goods. Playgrounds are quite often donated items such as record players. Though these may seem useful, they should be very carefully checked, as the reason for giving them away sometimes turns out to be that they are faulty – which may mean that they are very dangerous.

You should also be able to make a lot of use of scrounged materials for art and craft work – precisely how much depends on how imaginative you are at thinking up uses for what you obtain. If you have built up a good support network, there should not be much difficulty getting hold of old matchboxes, yoghurt cartons, egg boxes, old newspapers and the like, which can prove a useful way of involving people with the playground modestly but continuously. Contact local firms to see if they can provide offcuts of such materials as wood, leather, fabric and cardboard. In some cases, you may also be able to get hold of rejects and leftovers. Thus, if you have a button manufacturers nearby, you've got a source of a marvellous material for collages that can be used with children of an enormous range of ages and disabilities. Your nearest wastepaper merchants should be willing to supply you, free or very cheaply, with such materials as offcuts of card and unused ends of rolls of printing paper. (Or, if you have a large printer nearby, go directly to source!)

If you are lucky, there may be a scrap project in your area, set up as a resource for playgrounds and playgroups, which will save you a lot of the work of scrounging. You can find out by contacting your local play association or local authority Play and Recreation department.

Almost certainly you will still have to buy some of your art and craft equipment. But check whether your local education authority is willing to let you order materials such as paints and paper through them, as schools do: such an arrangement will save you both time and money. If they prove unco-operative, order from them indirectly, through a local school. If your playground is being used regularly by special schools, you may well find that they will be happy to donate some of the materials you need. (But be very wary of any suggestion that they get their pupils to bring from home specific materials for a particular purpose – such as ingredients for cooking. Though undoubtedly well-intentioned, such a suggestion runs a great risk of programming the kids' activities on the playground in a way that is entirely contrary to the basic philosophy of adventure play.)

With larger items of equipment, you should think carefully about how much use you have for them. Equipment you will only need occasionally may well be something you can borrow or hire. Your local youth service may have such items as projectors and camping equipment available for loan (and are also worth contacting as a possible source of grant aid). A school, youth club or scout group may be willing to lend their own equipment to you if you explain your need to them. Where a particular job needs doing, you may find that a local organisation may be willing to do it for you, providing both equipment and trained operators. Thus, when we were working on the Charlie Chaplin site, our local Territorial Army unit – which happens to be an engineering unit – turned up for a day with a couple of earth-movers. That might sound like a bit of good luck, but was really more than that: it only happened because we had contacted them in the first place, before we knew there was any possibility of them providing plant as well as labour. You may not have a TA engineering unit in your area, but that doesn't mean there is nobody else who would do the same job; it's up to you to go out and locate them.

The following list of types of scrap material and their possible uses on playgrounds was prepared by Pat Fairon of the Children's Scrap Project, London, for an article in the July 1983 issue of *Play Times*. It is, for obvious reasons, not exhaustive, but provides a good introduction to the enormous variety of possible practical applications for waste materials.

TYPES OF SCRAP	WHERE TO GET IT	HOW TO USE IT
Aluminium film cans	Film/TV studios	Drums; containers. Fill for sound/weight discrimination
Bark	Dead trees (countryside)	Collage; mosaic rubbings
Bamboo poles	Carpet stores	Frames; poles for wall hanging, etc; musical instruments; split and sand for struts for kites
Blueprint paper	Architects' offices	Print making
Bones	Butchers/restaurants	Print making; jewellery; sculpture
Bottle tops	Pubs	Counting games; collage; musical instruments, etc.
Bottles (glass)	Restaurants/wine bars/home	Musical instruments; storage
Bottles (plastic)	Home	Musical instruments (maracas); containers, etc.
Breeze blocks	Construction/demolition sites	Sculpture (carving)
Bricks	Construction/demolition sites	Constructions/shelving

TYPES OF SCRAP	WHERE TO GET IT	HOW TO USE IT
Candle stubs	Churches	Carving; wax resist drawing; batik
Cardboard boxes	Electrical appliance stores, supermarkets	Constructions; 'Wendy' type houses; furniture making, etc.
Carbon paper	Offices	Print making; tracing
Carpet scraps	Carpet stores, carpet layers	Quiet corners; collage; weaving
Ceramic tiles	Specialist tile shops	Mosaic; collage
Clay	Building excavations, river banks, etc.	Clay carving; pottery
Corks	Restaurants/wine bars	Construction/toy making; printing
Driftwood	Beach	Weird animals/carving, etc.
Egg cartons	Home	Too numerous to list
Egg shells	Home	Mosaic; collage
Fabric offcuts	Clothing manufacturers/ home	Collage; stuffed toys; 'dress making', etc.
Feathers	Poultry dealers	Collage; weaving; making pens
Felt scraps	Display departments of large stores	Felt boards; collage; stuffed toys; appliqué
Foam	Wholesale foam suppliers, furniture manufacturers	Sculpture; paintbrushes, etc.
Formica offcuts	Cabinet makers	Work surfaces for clay or plasticine
Greetings cards	Home	Collage; ornaments
Hessian	Display departments of large stores	Weaving games
Inner tubes	Garages servicing large trucks	Printmaking; drums; outdoor games

TYPES OF SCRAP	WHERE TO GET IT	HOW TO USE IT
Leather scraps	Leather goods manufacturers	Belts; purses; collage, etc.
Leaves	Countryside/parks	Printing; rubbing; collage, etc.
Lino offcuts	Lino layers	Printmaking
Magazines	Wholesale newsagents	Collage; montage; mosaic beads
Milk cartons	School cafeterias	Containers; moulds for candle making
Newspapers	Home	Protection for tables, etc., when doing 'dirty work'
Paint	Large department stores (display dept). Paint shops (returned or mismatched paint)	Painting constructions
Paper/card offcuts	Printers; waste paper collection depots	Too numerous to list
Pebbles	Beach	Mosaics; jewellery
Plastic fruit baskets	Greengrocers/ supermarkets	Constructions; storage; Easter Baskets
Sand	Beach	Play area
Seeds	Whole food stores; woods; parks	Mosaics; beads; musical instruments
Sheets (old)	Hospitals/hotels	Tie-die; batik; costumes, etc.
Shells	Beaches	Mosaics; constructions; 'toys'
Shoeboxes	Shoe shops	Storage; dioramas; weaving
String	Dispatch depot	Too numerous to list
Telephone cable spools	Post office	Tables; benches
Vegetables	Greengrocers/home	Carving; printing
Wallpaper samples	Wallpaper shops	Prints/rubbings; mosaics

TYPES OF SCRAP	WHERE TO GET IT	HOW TO USE IT
Wire	Dry cleaners (coat hangers); scrap metal merchants	Sculpture/musical instruments
Wood products (offcuts/shavings/sawdust)	Timberyards/furniture manufacturers	Too numerous to list

The same article warned against hazardous materials, pointing out that 'as a general rule all synthetic materials should be treated as basically hazardous until proved otherwise'. Some of the most dangerous materials include: *asbestos* in any form, as the fibres are toxic and accumulate in the body; *fibreglass* in any form, as the fibres are injurious to skin and lungs; *lead-based paints*, as lead is a cumulative poison; *expanded polystyrene* which, if cut or crumbled, produces small free-floating fragments which block the nasal passages and do not show up on X-rays, and if exposed to flame, drips sticky burning tar as well as giving off noxious fumes.

The article also pointed out that most useful waste falls into the category of potentially hazardous materials. Such useful but potentially hazardous materials include:

Paper products. Coated paper can have razor-sharp edges and may give off unhealthy fumes if burned. The paste in some pre-pasted wallpapers contains a fungicidal agent.

Wood products. Most timber is susceptible to splintering if abused; *plywood* often splits dangerously in the surface veneer if there is a poor joint; dust from some *hard woods* can cause an allergic reaction; *secondhand timber* generally contains nails somewhere – if it has been treated with creosote or painted (is the paint toxic?) its flash point may be reduced; *telegraph poles* marked 'S' or 'D' indicate S-Suspect, D-Defect.

Textiles. Synthetic textiles are usually very flammable, eg. synthetic fur fabric ignites easily and produces clouds of choking black smoke.

Plastics. Formica and perspex offcuts have sharp edges and corners capable of cutting quite deeply. Polythene bags can suffocate small children.

Polyurethane foam. In addition to being a fire risk some foams give off toxic fumes when alight. It should never be stored or used in large quantities (such as in stuffing cushions).

All potentially dangerous items, including not only scrounged scrap materials but also items such as cleaning materials and sharp or power-driven tools, should be safely stored in locked cupboards or workshops. A playground should always work on the assumption that kids are likely to experiment with whatever they can get at: as such experimentation is a central feature of playground activity, anything that is not safe for children to experiment with should not be left where they can get at it. This includes some items which it may be safe to let some, more responsible, children use on their own, or which may be used under the supervision of a playworker or other responsible adult.

Labour

It is important to realise that any playground needs a much larger workforce than can be supplied solely by its playworkers; its salaried playstaff provide the backbone of its labour force, but they need to be supplemented by other, unpaid workers if the playground is to operate at its full capacity and be as stimulating, ever-changing an environment as it should be. Such extra workers fall into three basic categories: volunteers; people on training schemes, such as those established for unemployed school-leavers; students on placement.

Volunteers are the most important of these three groups: they are likely to be the largest, and to include some people whose commitment to the playground will become a long-term one, so that they form part of the same network of support that you rely on for scrounging materials and for fundraising. It really is worth putting a good deal of work into building up and organising a good supply of voluntary help: properly used, they can take a great deal of the load off your playworkers, and extend the playground's scope in ways that would not otherwise be possible. This is particularly relevant where playgrounds are operating on restricted budgets, and can only afford to pay one or two playworkers: we know of some playgrounds whose staff would be quite unable to manage without the voluntary help they receive.

Tasks that volunteers can perform include: acting as drivers and escorts to transport children to and from the playground, as happens at the East London Handicapped Adventure Playground; structure-building and other construction work; general maintenance, clearing-up and cleaning; one-to-one work with severely disabled children; leading small groups in particular activities such as cooking or photography. People who have specific skills that will be of use to the playground are especially valuable: driving and maintenance provide two obvious examples of areas where such skills are called for. People who can relate well to children are *always* in demand. It is also useful to build up a list of contacts with people possessing more uncommon skills, who, while not working regularly as volunteers, may be willing to come in occasionally for a particular purpose. Thus, Charlie Chaplin playground has one contact who is a qualified welder, and sometimes comes in to repair broken pieces of equipment and do any other small welding jobs that may have arisen.

The work of accumulating voluntary helpers should start before a playground has even opened; there will certainly be plenty for volunteers to do at that stage – clearing the site, starting to build structures and getting the building ready for children to use. It is best, at this stage, to try to organise large sessions where a lot of people come in and spend a day working together: working on your own without any company is usually not much fun, and the playground is likely to be at a stage where even the people most closely involved with its development would benefit from a chance to get to know each other a little better. (Take care, however, if you still have contractors working on site, to arrange such working days in consultation with them, so that there is no interruption of their work.)

When looking for volunteers, start with people who have already shown an interest in, or a commitment to, the playground and its work: committee members and the people who got the project going in the first place; parents and teachers of children who use its facilities; interested friends of playworkers and of management committee members. Chelsea playground used to have members of its management committee coming in to run regular cooking sessions with groups of children – an activity which proved very popular both with the children and the committee members. An additional reason for encouraging committee members to work as playground volunteers, especially for this sort of activity – working with the children who use it – is that it makes them better committee members: they will have a better understanding of how the playground operates on a day-to-day level, and be more in touch with the difficulties that face the playworkers.

It is possible to go a stage further, and deliberately recruit volunteers from the local community. Local agencies, such as Voluntary Service Units, which exist to co-ordinate voluntary work, can be very helpful in this respect. You will make things simplest for them if you approach them with specific details of what needs doing and when ('We need someone to drive to the Cash and Carry once a fortnight to do a bulk buy of groceries'), rather than just a vague request for volunteers. Alternatively, you can start gaining people's interest in what the playground is doing by offering to give talks about its work to local schools, students' unions, tenants' associations and similar organisations, and then either use these sessions directly to make appeals for support on behalf of the playground, or follow them up later.

Any playground needs to have a clearly thought-out policy about how it uses volunteers, and how it responds to people who offer their services as volunteers. Potential volunteers need to be carefully vetted, especially if they are not known personally to members of the playground staff or committee: regrettably, organisations working with young people do sometimes attract people who are sexually interested in children; children who are mentally handicapped are particularly likely to be at risk. Although this is not a problem that crops up frequently, it is not one about which one can afford to be lax. Less seriously, there may be other individuals who are just not very suitable to work with children, such as someone who is prone to violent outbursts of temper which could prove distressing, particularly to children who are emotionally disturbed. It may even be somebody who is very experienced with children, but whose approach is not suited to adventure play. Whether tactfully to refuse the offer, or to find a job for them that won't involve much contact with children, is a decision that has to be made separately for each individual.

But don't be over-eager to class would-be volunteers as unsuitable, particularly once your playground has been going long enough to have developed a welcoming atmosphere of its own. For example: Chelsea playground used to have a volunteer who came in twice a week for a couple of hours to clean the kitchen. While she was there, the kitchen became very firmly her territory, and she ruled it with a strictness that would have been utterly inappropriate in a playworker. ('I've told you about this before, haven't I? If you want a drink of orange, ask me to get it for you, and don't come running across the floor I've just washed!' And woe betide any playworker who tried to make a cup of tea without permission . . .) The children using the playground simply got used to this approach, and learned to live with it. Some readers may be surprised to learn that we tend to see this contact with one individual's particular approach as beneficial to the children in question. Certainly there is a lot to be said in favour of an environment where children feel secure enough to be able to regard an adult's strictness simply as the personal foible of one individual, without feeling threatened by it.

Always bear in mind that people who offer to act as volunteers are doing the playground a favour, and deserve to be well treated; you need them more than they need you, and they should be able to feel that their presence is valued. When people offer their services, one of the playground staff should find the time to sit down with them and talk things over: how would they like to help? How much time do they want to give to the playground? Do they understand what would be involved? By the time the individual starts work in the playground, agreement should have been reached on what she is committing herself to; it makes sense to formulate this in fairly specific terms, so that the volunteer is not left at a loose end, wondering if there's anything for her to do or not. Obviously, it makes sense to try to find tasks for each volunteer that are appropriate to their abilities and personal interests. It is also helpful to try to fix regular times for each volunteer to come in; this enables the playground to plan their use of volunteers so that they can get the maximum benefit from their presence. It also means that children get to know their faces and are more likely to establish a relationship with them.

The playground should be prepared to support its volunteers in their work. They should be made to feel welcome, introduced to the people they will come into contact with, shown around the playground and given an explanation of how it operates, and be told about the basic philosophy of adventure play with handicapped children. (This does *not* apply only to volunteers who will be working directly with the children; if a volunteer is, for example, coming in to help with the cleaning, it is only civil to let them know how the mess gets caused in the first place.) It is a good idea for the playground to have a key worker responsible for voluntary helpers, so that they know who to go to if they have any queries or complaints. In some cases, playgrounds may wish, if funds permit, to pay expenses to regular volunteers, for items such as travel and meals.

Playstaff should consider whether they are willing to let volunteers come to team meetings. This can have advantages for both sides: volunteers gain a wider view of the playground's activities, and playworkers gain an extra perspective on the way the playground is running. It is not at all uncommon for volunteers to highlight issues that the workers have not yet become aware of. Above all, volunteer workers should be treated with respect: good volunteers make a major contribution to a playground's activities. It should be remembered also that people who become involved with a playground as volunteers may eventually progress to joining the playground's management committee, may prove a fruitful source of temporary workers for holiday projects or may even take the plunge and become full-time play workers.

Job-creation and training schemes funded by the Manpower Services Commission, Youth Training Services and similar bodies present a slightly different set of problems. These schemes can be an extremely valuable source of labour for playgrounds, particularly those which can not afford a large number of full-time staff. But they need to be handled with care. It must be remembered that these are *training* schemes; it is quite wrong to treat them solely as a source of cheap labour. Where playgrounds take on individual trainees, as with the schemes funded by YTS, they are also taking on a responsibility for giving them a certain amount of on-the-job training. This places an extra responsibility on playground staff, and it is therefore unwise for a playground to take on more than one or at most two such trainees at a time.

With schemes such as those funded by the MSC, which provide their own supervisors, there are fewer problems, and a number of playgrounds have taken very successful advantage of this way of increasing their labour force. Park View playground in Liverpool, for example, has an MSC scheme which runs the transport for the project. Charlie Chaplin has had a lot of help with construction and maintenance tasks, such as laying turf and building structures, from Community Industry, a local MSC project. The success of such ventures depends on careful planning. Playground staff must work out a programme of work to be done by the trainees, preferably of a fairly varied and interesting nature, and should meet the supervisors before the scheme starts, to discuss what facilities the playground will need to provide: will the trainees need to use the play building for making cups of tea and taking meal breaks, for example, and if so, how much disruption of the playground's regular activities is likely to be caused? Will the scheme need storage space for tools and materials? Much also depends on the quality of guidance and leadership given by the scheme's supervisor; play staff should satisfy themselves that they are confident that these will be adequate, and can legitimately expect to have a say in who is performing that role. As a badly-run scheme can cause a great deal of disruption while getting very little work done, all such details should be sorted out before final approval is given.

Handicapped adventure playgrounds tend to receive a substantial number of requests to take *students on placement*. This can provide a very attractive source of supplementary staff; when a playground is asked to accept a student placement, it is usually because the student has expressed an interest in the playground's work, so that his or her level of motivation and commitment to the playground's aims is likely to be much higher than that of, for example, the average YTS trainee. It often happens that people who initially come to a playground as students on placement are invited to return as paid temporary holiday workers, or even end up joining the playground's full-time staff. The fact that some colleges are willing to pay playgrounds to accept placements makes the proposition doubly attractive. It is of course possible for playgrounds to make it known to colleges that they are willing to take students on placement. If you wish to do this, check whether any local colleges run courses in such areas as social work or community work.

It should be remembered, however, that a student on placement is coming to the playground in order to learn how it operates. In accepting a placement, the playground also accepts responsibility for supervising and facilitating that process. Playground staff must therefore be prepared to spend time with the student explaining how the playground operates, discussing any issues that may have arisen during her work, and explaining the reasons behind actions that she has seen them take. The students may well be expected to produce a piece of written work as a result of her period on placement; if this is the case, workers must provide whatever co-operation she needs, answering her questions and being prepared to be interviewed about their work.

In general, if a playground is to make adequate use of the opportunities offered by the three categories of supplementary workers we have discussed, it needs to have an organised programme for doing so, and a thought-out policy about how it treats people who are not part of the full-time staff. So long as this basic planning is carried out, such workers should play a major part in the life of the playground.

Funding
A comprehensive guide to fund-raising would take up a whole book in itself. What follows are basic guidelines to how to go

about raising money; sources of more detailed information can be found in the reference section at the end of the book.

Money is the most obvious and necessary resource for a playground. Capital costs need to be raised to establish a project, and revenue costs found to keep it going thereafter. Committee members and all of those connected with the playground should be aware from the outset that fund-raising is a continuing activity that will never come to an end. It is one of the fundamental tasks that all committees of voluntary-run playgrounds have to take on. (We assume that if a local authority decides to establish a scheme of its own it will find the basic funds to do so from its own budget. Even so, playgrounds are likely to want to top that money up, especially for additional activities, such as taking a group of children camping for a weekend, and for purchasing extra equipment.)

Capital costs – the money needed to build and initially equip a playground – can vary enormously, and depend in part on the strength of the committee or organisation that is trying to start the project. In London, the Handicapped Adventure Playground Association has had the strength of organisation, experience and reputation to raise large sums of money to build its playgrounds: their last project, Charlie Chaplin playground in Lambeth, cost £220,000. But other projects, based in areas such as Gloucester and the Thames Valley, have found it far more difficult to raise the necessary funds and have had to pitch their costs at a much lower level – £30–40,000 – but one that was realistic for them to aim at. This of course means that 'cheaper' playgrounds have had to settle for less elaborate buildings, smaller quantities of equipment and, crucially, more limited numbers of staff.

There is no doubt that access to Urban Aid Grants and Inner City Partnership (ICP) money has made a great deal of difference to projects that are based in urban areas. These sources of money are unavailable to groups in more rural areas, and so restrict the amount of funds some projects can get from local authorities.

Nevertheless, it is important for all schemes to approach their local statutory bodies to see what scope there may be for grants, whether of a one-off nature or annually. Education, Amenities (often called Recreation) and Social Services Departments are all worth contacting for help and guidance, as are local Health Authorities. Remember that the financial year for local authorities runs from April to March, and bids for grants need to be in before a financial year begins; otherwise it may be necessary to wait a further year before applying. Statutory authorities do sometimes have surplus money left over towards the end of a financial year, which may be available for one-off grants; it is worth keeping an eye out for this. Lord Mayors' appeals and funds, though not strictly classifiable as statutory funding, are also worth looking out for. A good way of finding out about local authority or health authority finance is to get an officer, or elected representative, of either or both bodies on to the management committee. Their knowledge and expertise could save a lot of time and energy and be a good investment for long-term support.

The other source of money, once statutory sources have been explored, is the private business sector: business, industry and charitable trusts. Initially, it is necessary to research what organisations exist in your locality that could be potential donors. Use the library, Yellow Pages, business directories and Chambers of Commerce to find out where they are and who to contact. If possible, use the same technique as with statutory authorities: get a local business-person to sit on the project's committee. He will have an immediate knowledge which could prove invaluable. To locate charitable trusts, use the *Directory of Grant Making Trusts*, which is available in most large libraries. (Many such trusts can only give money to organisations that are registered as charities; if your group is not registered, it is normally quite acceptable to channel such donations through another group that is, and which supports your aims enough to be willing to help.)

Another essential contact to be made in this area is with local businessmen's clubs, such as Rotary and Lions clubs. Don't be put off by idiosyncratic names such as the Grand Order of Water Rats: such organisations are often of immense help and many schemes, of all sorts, would not be operating today if it were not for their help. When approaching local concerns for funding, it is important that face-to-face contact is made, and that communication is not just through letter or telephone.

You must also develop a fund-raising strategy. This might include the creation of a fund-raising group as part of the main management committee. Such a group would deal with ideas such as publicity materials, the need to visit potential sponsors, the best time to approach people, and of course the organisation of the group's own fund-raising activities, such as sponsored walks, raffles, jumble sales and summer fairs.

Two important points need to be considered in any fund-raising programme. First, are people being approached for one-off grants, such as for specific pieces of equipment, or are they being asked to give regular annual grants which contribute to revenue funding, such as money towards staff salaries? The former are always more popular with sponsors, partly because they don't commit themselves to so much, but also because, if their money is paying for one particular item, they can envisage more clearly how much good it will be doing. So, whenever you ask for donations, try to name the purpose they will be used for as precisely as possible.

The second point to bear in mind is that it can be dangerous to explore and exploit all the local businesses and trusts in one go. A project needs constant funding, and if all potential resource contacts are exhausted quickly it will be more difficult to generate funds as the playground matures, because everyone will feel they have already given. This applies particularly to schemes based outside large conurbations, in areas where communities and businesses operate on a smaller scale. Some projects have found that they are constantly trying to tap the same people for money, ranging from grants to selling raffle tickets, and are finding it more and more difficult to get a good response.

The concept of 'joint funding', increasingly being used by voluntary projects, is worth considering, particularly in relation to staff posts which are the single most costly item within a project's budget. Joint funding can take a number of different forms, such as two departments within a local authority contributing equal amounts, two neighbouring authorities sharing the costs of a project which will serve both areas, the local health authority and local government authority contributing, or money from private sources being matched with statutory funds. (The case history of Charlie Chaplin playground in Chapter 11 describes in more detail an example of such joint funding.) This is an area that needs considering within any fund-raising strategy.

The idea of different voluntary bodies taking part in joint fund-raising activities is another idea to explore. Such activities could range from shared summer or Christmas fairs to jointly organised sponsored events, which often require large numbers of people to organise them. To get into this network, committees need to be aware of what other bodies exist within their area. Councils for Voluntary Service, which are usually based on borough, town, city or county areas should be able to help here.

Many people coming new into the voluntary sector find the prospect of fund-raising a daunting one, particularly when groups start to talk in terms of thousands of pounds. It is important not to get too despondent. It is equally important to be realistic about what can be done and the length of time it will take. This is why a fund-raising strategy is important. A number of playgrounds now in operation took several years to raise the necessary money, and several not yet in existence are still working hard to raise the required amount. They have learnt to be patient and not give up hope. In this time they may also have had to revise their initial plans, even to the extent of looking for different, and cheaper, sites and buildings to develop. If there is sufficient enthusiasm and belief in the philosophy of adventure play a project will be established.

Some thought should be given to annual budgets. It is useful for schemes to draw up budget proposals for the coming year if for no other reason than to concentrate people's minds on how much money is necessary to keep a project going, and how determined fund-raising activities need to be. Every year voluntary projects have to present accounts for audit and approval under charitable law, and these can be used as a basis for predicting future income and expenditure. Budgets encourage good housekeeping, particularly if schemes are operating on shoestring finance. To operate such an idea successfully, a good committee treasurer is needed to plan out and monitor its progress, and judge whether alterations are necessary as the financial year progresses.

Another use for well-kept annual accounts and budget proposals is when local authorities or private sources of funding are being approached for support. Well-presented financial statements show good practice, which people will respect and respond to, as an indication that the money they are being asked to donate is not likely to be wasted through straightforward financial mismanagement. And in asking for help from statutory agencies a budget, plus the past year's income and expenditure statements, will be required as a matter of course.

When organising fund-raising of your own, work out carefully whether the amount of money you're likely to make is worth the amount of work you will have to put in. It's not worth spending months organising a jumble sale, for example, if you only end up making fifteen or twenty pounds. The more you can delegate the work to other people, the easier it is to fund-raise successfully. The big advantage of a sponsored walk, for example, is that the people who are taking part raise their own sponsorship money. What's even better is if you can persuade other people to organise fund-raising events of their own in aid of your project. If you can persuade a local pub to 'adopt' you, they may raise a great deal of money for you and (a very important factor) have a lot of fun doing it. Successful fund-raising has a lot in common with scrounging for materials, in the sense that you need to build up a strong support network – even if people do no more than sell a few pounds' worth of raffle tickets once a year, you can make a lot of money if you have enough people doing it for you. (But if you want to organise something like this, such as a Christmas Draw, where you sell tickets to the general public, remember that you need to have a lotteries licence, obtainable from your local Town Clerk's department. This does not apply to an ordinary raffle, where tickets are sold only to people attending one particular event.)

7 Equipment

A playground's choice of equipment – a category that covers everything from spare fuses to play structures – is a major factor in its ability to operate successfully. If a playground is inadequately equipped, it will be less interesting and exciting for children to use, and more limiting for severely disabled children in particular; it will be a more dangerous environment for children to play in and staff to work in; it will place unnecessary and unfair pressures on its playworkers, who will find themselves forced to spend extra time working directly with children to compensate for the lack of opportunities that would be present on a better-equipped playground, while actually having less time to do so. While inanimate pieces of equipment can never take the place of the human contact that is a vital element of adventure playground work, they can vastly increase the range of opportunities available to children and ensure that playworkers spend as much time as possible working directly with children. This is particularly true of adventure playgrounds for handicapped children, which do not necessarily have the option of adopting the relatively rough-and-ready approach originally envisaged by Sørensen, which served many early conventional adventure playgrounds well.

It is important, therefore, that handicapped adventure playgrounds be prepared to devote substantial time and money to making sure that they have an adequate range of equipment both for use by children (toys, bicycles, art and craft materials, play structures) and for background tasks such as maintenance and administration. If you are setting up a new playground you can reasonably expect equipment to be, after the cost of site and building, the largest item of your capital budget. You should draw up careful estimates and, if possible, seek advice from existing playgrounds at an early stage, so that you can produce rough costings before you are ready to plan your needs in detail; but don't leave detailed planning until the last minute: once you have worked out your precise needs, you may, if you have left time to do so, be able to save quite a lot of money by persuading people to donate items of equipment, new or second-hand.

Follow the procedure suggested in the chapter on starting a playground, and work out, area by area, what will be needed for each part of the playground. In the longer term, you should budget for replaceable items, such as art and craft materials, maintenance of existing equipment (and its eventual replacement when it gets beyond the point where it is worth maintaining) and, if possible, the gradual acquisition of items that you can not afford when starting out. You will probably find it necessary to assign priorities to your equipment needs, ranging from the essential, such as fire extinguishers, to items you would very much like to have but can manage without for the time being, such as a darkroom or soft play area. Assigning these priorities is a very important piece of planning, because many of your decisions will affect the individual nature of your playground. In the examples just cited, you may give particular priority to a darkroom if one of your workers possesses particular experience of photographic work with children with disabilities. Or you may feel that the number of children using your playground who have relatively severe mobility limitations is such that a soft play area would be particularly valuable.

You should beware, however, of jumping to too many conclusions before the playground is open. It is easy for an inexperienced management committee, particularly if they start purchasing equipment before they have appointed their playstaff, to spend a lot of money on expensive pieces of equipment designed specifically for disabled children, and then find that many of them are very rarely used, or just not suitable for an adventure playground environment. Consult the playworkers on other handicapped adventure playgrounds and, if in doubt, put the money aside and wait until the playground is running; it is much easier to tell what equipment will really be useful once the playground is being used by children. In general, it is a mistake to assume that large amounts of highly specialised equipment are needed to cope with the fact that the children using the playground have disabilities. Play facilities for children with disabilities should be geared to the fact that they are children, who have the same need to play as other children, and not primarily to the existence of their disabilities. Many of the most useful pieces of equipment for children who are physically handicapped are very simple ones: the foam wedge or canvas sling that allows a severely disabled child to lie on his stomach and play with something on the floor; the smock or overall that allows a child with cerebral palsy to paint a picture without worrying about splashing her clothes. Bear in mind also that to think of disability solely in terms of wheelchairs and other signs of physical handicap is a gross piece of stereotyping: many of the children on most handicapped adventure playgrounds are fairly physically able, and even those who are not will not benefit from an approach that concentrates on their assumed inabilities rather than seeking ways of helping them use their real abilities.

One essential quality of playground equipment is that it be robust, because it gets a lot of hard usage, particularly as children do not always use toys and other pieces of equipment in the way that the manufacturers may have intended. Obviously, certain items bought for specialised purposes, such as darkroom equipment, need to be reserved for the purpose for which they were intended, but these should be kept in storage and only brought out when they are going to be used. Otherwise, children should feel free to play with the playground's equipment in whatever way – within reason! – takes their fancy, without being hemmed in by rules. This does of course mean that some pieces of equipment, particularly those that have been donated and were not originally bought for rough treatment, will have a limited life, but one just has to accept that there is a fairly rapid turnover of such objects on a playground. The flexibility of imagination that finds a new use for a piece of equipment that was manufactured for some quite different purpose is one of the very qualities that a playground exists to encourage. Play-workers should bear in mind that, when children's play takes unexpected forms, there are often lessons to be learnt: is the expected use of that piece of equipment dull and boring? is the child using an unlikely instrument because there isn't anything better for the purpose available on the playground – a possible pointer to the need for some other piece of equipment? or is it just the old story of adults having wrong expectations of children, based on inadequate understanding of their needs? Such questions, based on trust in the seriousness of children's decisions, are what led Sørensen to formulate the idea of junk playgrounds in the first place; it is important that we do not stop asking them.

The possibility that play equipment may be used in a variety of different ways should in fact be one of the criteria used when choosing it. Good play equipment is open-ended, lending itself to a variety of different purposes and offering the child a range of possibilities rather than narrowing them down. This does not necessarily mean that equipment has to be expensive: a lot of playgrounds have one or two old supermarket shopping trollies, which have proved extremely popular and adaptable. Children use them to ride in, to push around the playground, to transport materials from one part of the playground to another, to push each other around in or to run races with. They will also stand up to a lot of rough use, and are in any case quite easy to replace.

Because playground equipment gets such heavy use, it is important, when buying more expensive items, to consider, not only how robust they are, but how easy they will be to maintain. What is likely to go wrong with any particular item? How often are the problems likely to occur? How easy will they be to repair? Will special tools be needed to do it? If spare parts will be needed, how easy will they be to get hold of, and how much are they likely to cost? All these questions need to be considered, and the answers to them weighed up against the cost and potential usefulness to the playground, before you purchase any major item of equipment. You should also consider, of course, what benefit the children using the playground are likely to get from any particular piece of play equipment and whether there might be a simpler way of accomplishing the same end; this is an especially relevant question when considering the purchase of elaborate items of 'adapted' equipment.

In planning your equipment needs, you also need to consider the question of storage space, of which you will require a great deal; many playgrounds have discovered that it is very easy indeed to underestimate the amount of space that will be needed for storage, especially once a playground has been going for some while and has added considerably to the equipment it had when it first opened. If you are planning a purpose-built play building, make sure that you impress very firmly upon your architects that you would rather have too much storage space than too little; we have not known a playground yet that had too much.

Playground storage can be divided into two categories: that which is directly available to children, and that which is not. The first category, covering all the things such as toys and games which you want all the children using the playground to be able to pick up and start using whenever they wish, can be dealt with by providing a lot of shelving around the main play area, supplemented by free-standing items such as a large box or hamper of dressing-up clothes.

You will also need storage space that is not open to children. In particular, it is essential, as a basic safety precaution, that you have lockable cupboards or stores for items such as bleach and other cleaning materials, tools (especially those which are either sharp or power-operated) and anything else of a potentially dangerous nature. Do not forget that such facilities need to be backed by a clearly-thought-out safety policy: there's not much point in having lockable cupboards for dangerous materials if workers or volunteers leave them open for children to get into.

You should also, if possible, be able to lock away your stocks of materials that you buy in bulk. For each day's activity, put out adequate amounts of basic materials such as powder paints, plus whatever you need for any structured activity you may have planned. Such a policy reduces wastage to a tolerable level and also makes things simpler for those children who might be overwhelmed by too great a choice of activities of a particular kind. (Don't worry about the possibility that some children might want to do an activity you have not brought out the materials for; you can bring out extra materials and equipment when they are asked for.)

Remember also to have adequate storage space for the various items of equipment that are normally in use on the playground during the day, such as ropes and mobile equipment. It might not seem important to have space set aside for items which are normally only brought into the building when it is not being used by children. Your cleaner will soon tell you different, however, if you are in the habit of simply dumping them on the playroom floor! You should also remember that there will be occasions when the weather is unfit for outside play: it is not a good idea to have the inside of your play building cluttered up with outdoor equipment at the very times when all the children in the playground will be playing indoors.

Mobile Equipment

On almost any adventure playground for handicapped children, the type of equipment that gets the most use is mobile equipment such as tricycles, bicycles, scooters, pedal go-karts and pull-along trucks. You only have to walk into such a playground, in any but the very worst weather, to see children pedalling around, on their own or with other children – sometimes several of them crammed precariously on to a single long-suffering tricycle, or being pulled along by an even more long-suffering playworker – all over the playground and up and down the structures.

The very fact that children so obviously enjoy playing on these pieces of equipment should be sufficient argument to demonstrate the importance of budgeting for them from the very start. But trikes, go-karts and the rest are valuable for other reasons as well. They are clearly beneficial to the children using them insofar as they provide vigorous outdoor exercise in an exciting and enjoyable way; they also develop children's sense of balance and give them an experience of speed. If you have chosen the equipment carefully, it should include something for all but the most severely disabled children who use the playground to use *on their own*, without needing the support of an adult helper.

But perhaps the most important aspect of mobile equipment is that it provides many children whose mobility or physical strength is limited, with a large degree of extra independence, enabling them to explore the farthest points of the playground on their own, and to play with other children on relatively equal terms. This applies even to children whose leg movement is so limited that they are unable to pedal or even push a bicycle along: they can use an adapted tricycle that is pedalled by hand. Another type of adapted trike has especially low gearing, so that it can be used by children whose legs are too weak to pedal an ordinary tricycle – who, of course, get a valuable chance to exercise their leg muscles in the process.

Bikes and trikes also encourage independence in children who are more physically able. The more nervous child who has just started using a playground may feel a little intimidated by its size at first, and tend not to venture very far away from the play building. Because it is by definition impossible to stay in one place while riding a bike or pedalling a go-kart, such a child may well, particularly if playing with another child, venture farther afield than he might have felt ready to do on foot. (Once he has crossed the wide-open spaces for the first time, it is of course perfectly possible that he will become interested by what he finds, and leave the bike so that he can go down a slide, paddle in the pool or have a go on a swing, with the result that his initial nervousness of this unexplored terrain will be quite forgotten by the end of the afternoon.)

The warning given earlier about being wary in your choice of specially adapted equipment is particularly applicable to mobile equipment: some adapted bicycles are very valuable indeed; others, particularly if they are not sturdy enough for everyday use and so have to be kept aside for children with the particular disability for which they are intended, are hardly ever used. Which is which depends partly on what children use your playground. Consult other playgrounds, and also observe for yourself which are most popular with those playgrounds' children.

Mobile equipment tends to need a lot of maintenance, partly because it gets used so heavily, even by playground standards. When purchasing it, you should try to choose items that are as simple and sturdy as possible, unlikely to go wrong very often and simple to repair when they do. Thus, you should always, as far as possible, try to choose bikes and trikes that have solid rubber tyres: pumping up tyres and repairing punctures can take up a lot of a playworker's time, which would be better spent in other ways. Charlie Chaplin playground has two of the low-geared bikes mentioned earlier; they are popular with kids using the playground, but, because they have large inflatable tyres, they spend more time in the workshop waiting to be repaired than they do being used by children. One playground we know got so fed up with bikes being out of service because of punctures that they simply removed all inflatable tyres and let the kids ride around on the metal rims of the wheels – a rather noisy solution, perhaps, but it did at least ensure that the bicycles remained in fairly regular use.

It is worth building up a stock of spares for use in maintaining mobile equipment. Try as far as possible to anticipate what you're likely to need so that you don't have to keep a bicycle out of service for weeks or months on end while you wait for a small replacement part to arrive (although, if you've chosen your equipment carefully, you shouldn't have much that it is difficult to get spares for). Make particularly sure that you have a good supply of the minor parts such as nuts and bolts and split pins that are most likely to need replacing. And when a piece of mobile equipment does reach the end of its working life, don't throw it away until you've stripped it of all the parts, such as bicycle chains and wheels, which can be cannibalised to add to your stock of spares.

Don't forget, either, that damage to mobile equipment can be partly the result of bad storage. If your storage space is so limited that you have to pile bikes, trikes and go-karts on top of one another, and pull the whole pile apart again before you put them out in the morning, you may well be shortening the usable life of this equipment. Try, if possible, to have enough space to leave each piece of equipment standing on its own piece of floor. Keep a check list of what pieces you possess, and make sure they have all been put away before you close the playground: tricycles and go-karts end up in the most extraordinary places, left there by children who have become interested in something else and wandered off – or even, on occasion, deliberately carried by some little horror to places to which they could never be ridden.

It is especially worthwhile having pieces of mobile equipment which can be used by several children at one time, thus encouraging them to play together, which can be particularly valuable for children who have limited experience of mixing socially with others of their own age. We strongly recommend the low wooden pull-along truck manufactured by Bowley and Coleman Trucks Ltd – an exceptionally sturdy piece of equipment, whose popularity with playground users is partly due to its versatility: a single child can either pull it around empty or use it for transporting items, such as the materials for building a den, from one part of the playground to another; two or more children can take turns to pull each other around, or, if they're in luck, persuade a playworker or some other hapless adult to do the pulling, with all of them squeezed into it together.

Where a playground is operating on limited resources, and does not have much money to spare to buy expensive pieces of manufactured equipment, items of mobile equipment are relatively easy to raise funds for: most of them fall within the price range that could be covered by a single successful fund-raising event, and they are attractive to private donors because it is easy to imagine children having fun with them. It could be well worth approaching local businesses and other organisations to suggest that they might consider purchasing a particular adapted tricycle, for example.

It should not be thought, however, that only expensive items of manufactured equipment are any use to a playground in this context. We have already quoted the example of the super-market trolley. Playgrounds should also consider making some bits of equipment themselves: it is not difficult, for example, to make a version of the traditional soap-box cart, adapted so it will securely hold a child who has limited mobility. Reduced to its most basic version, it would consist of what would effectively be a sturdy wooden box mounted on wheels or castors, with a bit of rope by which to pull it along.

One particularly intriguing idea comes from SKIP (Sheffield Children's Integrated Play – see the chapter on Integration), who suggest that it is useful to have one or two spare wheelchairs, to be used for fun by children who do not have disabilities which normally require them to use wheelchairs. A report on their first playscheme commented that, 'For the able-bodied it was a great novelty to play games in wheelchairs or sitting on the ground. Spare wheelchairs for able-bodied children to play in were one of the greatest aids to integration.' Though this suggestion was made primarily in relation to integrated projects, we see no reason why it should not work equally well in a handicapped adventure playground; indeed, as happens with other pieces of equipment, we are sure that in the environment of an adventure playground children would find all sorts of new ways of using them.

Shopping trolleys, boxes on wheels, old wheelchairs . . . whatever next? That, we're afraid, is yet another question for you to answer for yourselves. Your ingenuity can solve your playground's needs. Put it to work.

Tools

We have known a number of projects which either under-estimated the quantity and variety of tools they would need, or tried to economise by buying only a bare minimum. It proved to be a mistake in every case. A playground has to have an extensive set of tools for a variety of purposes and there is no way around that need. For a project that is operating on limited funds the need is even more crucial, because they will have to do more of their own maintenance and are more likely to be making a lot of their own equipment rather than purchasing it. It might seem that you can at least manage without buying drain rods, for example, until the time comes when you actually need to use them; but has it occurred to you that a blocked drain could – if it means your lavatories are out of action, or leads to severe flooding – mean that the playground will have to close until it's sorted out? In the long term, it makes sense not to take that sort of risk.

The tools a playground should possess can be roughly divided into five categories. In the first place, every adventure playground needs a good selection of tools for structure building. Even if a playground has been able to persuade someone else to build their structures for them, playworkers will need to carry out maintenance, and should also be constantly changing and extending the playground's structures: a good adventure playground is not a static environment. These tools should include heavy hammers and saws – several of each, as structure building tends to be a group activity; digging equipment, plus ropes and pulleys, for use in erecting telegraph poles; an auger plus, if at all possible, a power drill, for boring bolt-holes; a long (25–30 foot) ladder; a comprehensive set of heavy-duty spanners in both AF and metric sizes; sledge-hammers – both heavy (28lb) and lighter ones suitable for demolishing old structures, when staff may be working above shoulder height; a spirit level, for getting telegraph poles upright and levelling joists and floors; a set of large heavy-duty chisels for making joints; nail-bars, for de-nailing recycled timber. Buy bowsaws rather than conventional joiners' handsaws; blades are easily blunted on the recycled timber used for most structure-building, and need to be replaced frequently. Bowsaws also have the subsidiary advantage that they let two people share the work of any particularly heavy sawing job.

It is absolutely essential that appropriate safety measures are observed when structures are being built. This means that workers must be equipped with the right tools for whatever job they are doing, and that the playground must possess safety equipment such as protective clothing. Some items, such as sturdy boots, need to be bought to fit the individual; it is normal practice for playgrounds to give workers a clothing grant to cover such items. Unless the playground possesses or has access to scaffolding, it is useful to possess a climbing harness and ropes for use when working at heights; though long ladders are convenient, many playworkers take far more risks than they should when using them.

If, as they should be, your structures are being bolted together, you will need a power drill. (It is possible to use an auger, but to do so is a dreadful waste of your playworkers' time.) You will also need a half-inch bit a foot or more long: the easiest way of fixing joists to telegraph poles is to position them temporarily with nails, and then drill both joist and pole; ideally, therefore, you need a bit long enough to go through two joists and a telegraph pole. It is preferable to have an industrial drill for such purposes, but it is possible to make do with a lighter one. If you are worried about the cost of a power drill, bear in mind that, in terms of the saving in playworkers' time alone, it will pay for itself within a few days. It will also prove useful for a lot of other playground tasks, such as putting up shelves. A portable circular saw, though less vitally necessary than a power drill, is another very useful labour-saving device. But if you are going to buy power tools, you must ensure that anybody who will be using them has been trained to do so; consult an appropriate play organisation or the local Health and Safety Inspectorate for details of where to find such training. You should also check your insurance policy to see if it lays down any particular conditions relating to the use of power tools on the playground.

The second category of tools a playground needs are those for maintaining equipment, and mobile equipment in particular. As well as the spares discussed in the last section of this chapter, you need a range of tools from small spanners – again, in both metric and non-metric sizes – to welding gear. (The latter, like power tools, should only be used by people who have been trained in its use: you do not necessarily need to buy welding gear so long as you have access to it, so check whether a local play association, or another local playground, can lend or hire you the equipment.) Precisely what tools you need for this purpose depends on what equipment you possess, and will have to be worked out accordingly.

You also need to buy a lot of tools for use in maintaining your play building. This is probably the category that needs to be most carefully planned out, because the range of tasks that may arise is large, and varies according to the nature of your particular building: it is easy to forget about some aspects of maintenance until the need actually arises. Try, therefore, to work out, in as methodical a fashion as possible, what maintenance your play building is going to require. Start by working out the everyday needs, which should be a fairly straightforward operation: you will obviously need cleaning equipment, for example – brooms, mops, buckets and so forth. Then look ahead and envisage what is likely to be needed in the future. Are you ever likely to want a roof ladder, for example? Once you have worked out all the possible disasters that might occur, decide how urgent a problem they are likely to present. Might they be, as with the blocked drains mentioned earlier, major crises that will have to be dealt with as rapidly as possible, so that if specialised tools are needed you ought to possess them in advance? Or will they simply be matters which you can worry about when the time comes? And how likely are they to occur? Careful use of such a procedure should enable you to work out a detailed list of the tools you will need and to attach priorities to them: everyday use (mops, buckets, brooms, screwdrivers, pliers, hammers); less frequent but regular use (paint brushes, saws, chisels); infrequent, but urgently needed when the problem arises (drain rods, spare fuses). A well-equipped playground should possess an adequate supply of all of these, and will presumably build up a stock of other, less essential, items as occasions for their use arise.

You must also, as a legal requirement, buy fire extinguishers and fire blankets. You should seek the advice of your local Fire Prevention Officer, who will tell you what you need and where it should be placed. When you arrange for the installation of this equipment sign a maintenance contract to ensure that it is kept in working order; make sure, also, that if any of the extinguishers are ever used they are automatically inspected and refilled afterwards. Always keep a fire drill notice prominently displayed. Further details about necessary fire precautions can be found in the NPFA's *Towards a Safer Adventure Playground*.

The fourth category of tools a playground requires consists of those needed for outside work. Many of these, such as spades, picks, grubbing mattocks and a wrecking bar, will be the same digging implements used in putting up structures. You will also need a supply of gardening tools; quite how many will depend on whether you have a garden area as such. It would be a very dull playground that possessed no wild areas at all, partly because there would be much less wildlife on such a site, but there will still be occasional work to be done: to clear overhanging foliage away from a path, cut down nettles or dig up some poisonous plant that has taken root.

The final category consists of tools to be used by children. It is as well to buy a selection of tools specifically for this purpose. These should include such items as small hammers that can be used by younger children or those who, because of their disability, would have difficulty using a heavier hammer. Remember that this may apply not only to building tools, for use in constructing dens and camps, but also to such items as gardening implements and paintbrushes. A further reason for having a separate set of tools is that when used by children they will inevitably get fairly rough treatment, and may sometimes be lost. It makes sense to safeguard the tools that are being kept for maintenance tasks by keeping them separate.

Inflatables and Soft Play

Inflatables are a very popular piece of play equipment on any adventure playground, and are particularly valuable to a handicapped adventure playground because of the oppor- tunities for exciting play they give to children who have limited mobility. Although they need not be regarded as essential, we would suggest that an inflatable comes high up on your list of pieces of equipment to be acquired when you can spare the money or persuade someone to donate them. They can be bought ready-made, in which case they cost several hundred pounds, or can possibly be made by playworkers with the help of expert advice in design and construction, a service that is sometimes offered by play organisations or local resource groups: if this way of doing it appeals to you, contact your local play association to find out if there is anyone in your area who offers this service.

An inflatable should always be used on grass, or some other

relatively soft surface, and should not be so high that a child falling off it risks injury. Even so, it must be under constant supervision when in use: it would be easy for children playing unsupervised to become so boisterous that someone could be injured by being accidently jumped on: at one playground, a worker injured her back when a child jumped on to her while she was lying with another child on the inflatable. Children using it should take their shoes off and remove any sharp objects from their pockets – these measures being designed to protect the children as well as the inflatable. Nor should it be used by too many children at one time. Safety becomes a particularly crucial factor when the inflatable is being put up or taken down: a child may fail to realise that if you jump on a half-full inflatable it will not contain enough air to support you, and you will go crashing to the ground. These tasks should preferably be carried out when there are no children on the playground.

Playworkers should bear in mind that an inflatable can be used in a variety of ways. It can be a source of exciting, boisterous activity, and can equally well be used to provide a very gentle type of play with severely physically handicapped children. (Obviously, it is neither practical nor sensible to try to have the two going on at the same time.) It can also be used for imaginative play, as where a worker or volunteer takes a group of children on a 'magic carpet ride', telling them a story and providing them with actions to perform to go along with it.

A certain amount of care must be taken over the way the inflatable is stored; if it has got wet while outside, make sure it is dried out before being folded up and put away; otherwise, the damp is likely to affect the glue that holds it together, or cause the plastic to smell or become mouldy. You should possess glue and spare material for repairing punctures and split seams.

The indoor equivalent of the inflatable is the soft play area, which is normally a separate room, whose walls and floor are lined with foam, containing a number of large foam shapes. Pieces of soft play equipment can be found in the catalogues of a number of toy manufacturers and suppliers. This is one case where it is important to use commercially made equipment unless you have competent professional advice, as foam is a serious potential fire hazard – most types of foam catch light easily, and exude poisonous fumes when they burn – and therefore needs to be well protected by fire resistant material. A further advantage of such materials is that they can be easily cleaned; this needs to be done regularly.

We have seen several examples of such soft play areas – at the old Chelsea Playground, the East London Handicapped Adventure Playground and the playground at St Lawrence's Hospital, Caterham, and feel that they provide an admirable form of activity, particularly suitable for children with limited mobility. Again, shoes should be taken off, and the number of children using the area at any one time should be limited.

A lot of playgrounds simply do not have enough indoor space to provide a facility such as this, even on a fairly limited scale. But if that is not the case, we suggest that serious thought be given to creating a soft play area.

Structures

The most important equipment on any adventure playground is its play structures, whose platforms, walkways, ramps, ladders, slides and swings are purpose-built to give children the opportunity to play adventurously, developing their physical capabilities and building self-confidence. Good structures should be designed and built by a playground's workers to the particular needs of the children using that playground.

Play structures will inevitably look dangerous to some outsiders, since one of their functions is to give children an opportunity to climb, and to develop their concepts of height and space. (One thing that can sometimes be observed on handicapped adventure playgrounds is that a child who has got to the top platform of a structure will stay there spending a lot of time just looking around, relishing the previously unknown experience of being up above the everyday world.) It may therefore sometimes be necessary for playground workers to reassure parents or teachers. Such reassurance is justified: adventure playgrounds have a far better safety record than conventional swings-and-asphalt playgrounds, partly because it is generally recognised in the adventure play movement that safety is a major consideration in running a playground – particularly when putting up structures.

Building structures is a relatively skilled job, which should not be undertaken without training in appropriate building methods and equipment, and a good knowledge of the safety guidelines and legislation covering structure-building. A number of short training courses for playworkers are available: contact your local or regional play association or regional Play Development Officer for details. (See the Reference Section for details of relevant publications.)

Safety guidelines need to be followed at three separate stages. First, in the design of structures: are there secure railings and hand-rails where needed? are the materials being used adequate for the purpose, and free from nails, splinters and sharp edges? are they well-sited, so that, for example, no child is likely to run into the path of a swing? And, most important of all, are they solid enough? A useful rule of thumb is that a structure should be able to support as many children as it has room for, all jumping up and down at the same time. If there is any doubt at all whether a structure will be strong enough, DON'T BUILD IT! Or, if it's already built, pull it down – it *has* been known in the past for a child to be killed when a badly-built structure collapsed.

Secondly, in the actual building: all workers involved, including volunteers, should be familiar with the relevant safety guidelines and equipped with appropriate protective clothing such as steel-toed boots and safety helmets. It may be possible to let kids join in the work at some stages – a valuable chance for them to get involved in adult activity, something that children are increasingly denied in the modern city – but a great deal of common sense and forethought needs to be used. Thus, for example, if children are going to help with painting the structures, emulsion paint should be used rather than gloss, which doesn't come off with soap and water.

Thirdly, in maintenance. Any wear and tear should be fixed before it becomes dangerous: a continuous watch should be kept for minor damage such as wood splintering or nails becoming loosened by vibration. Playstaff should be on the lookout for weaknesses in design that may be shown up by the way kids use the structures – the sides of a slide may need to be raised, or a swing may need to be repositioned. A regular health and safety check of the entire playground should be held at least once every six months, with any faults that are revealed being promptly sorted out. Ropes should be taken down and stored under cover every night, and checked for possible fraying at the same time. Make sure that the correct knots are used for the purposes to which ropes are put; Scout Association publications can be a useful source of information for this.

Your playground should possess a copy of the NPFA's *Towards a Safer Adventure Playground*, and your staff and management should be familiar with the contents of this essential guide to playground safety, which contains a substantial section on structures. A useful introduction to health and safety practices for playgrounds is also provided by the tape/slide show on the subject produced by LAPA. Playground management committees should remember that it is, ultimately, their responsibility to ensure that correct health and safety procedures are followed on their playground, and that they could be held legally responsible for any failure to follow them: if they do not know in detail what this responsibility consists of, they'd better find out in a hurry.

The first stage in designing structures, especially on a new playground, is to plan the layout of the site, bearing in mind how the kids are likely to use them. For example, structures that are likely to be used by younger, less able and less confident children should be placed away from those that will attract older and more able-bodied children, whose more boisterous play might prove intimidating; such smaller structures are probably best sited fairly near the play building where timid kids will feel more secure – they will go farther afield as their confidence grows. Structures that encourage more adventurous play should be laid out so that it is easy for playworkers to keep an eye on them. Use should be made of the existing landscape: if you want to erect a jumping-off platform for a high swing, can it be placed on an existing mound? Larger swings should be placed so that other children are not likely to run into their path and get hurt;

Sand . . .

Photo Tilly Odell

. . . and water

Photos Tilly Odell

Inflatables

Photo Tilly Odell

One-to-one

Photo Patrick Sutherland

tructures . . .

Photo Tilly Odell

. . . and swings

Photo Tilly Odell

Photo Patrick Sutherland

Trikes, trucks and go-karts

Right photo Bob Bray
Below photo Tilly Odell

Animals

Photo Bob Bray

Photo Tilly Odell

Indoor Play

Photo Bob Bray

Photo Bob Bray

Pho
Bol

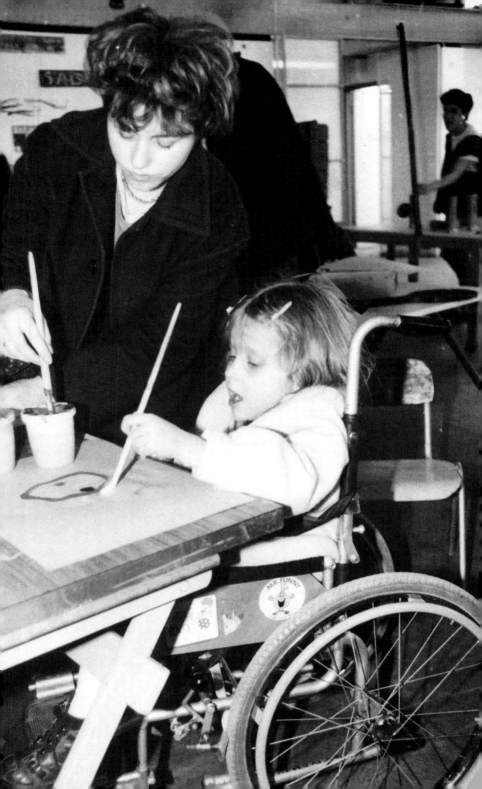

Photo Patrick Sutherland

Photo Patrick Sutherland

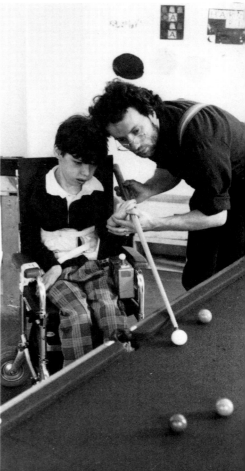

Photo Patrick Sutherland

Photo Patrick Sutherland

Dressing up . . .

Photo Bob Bray

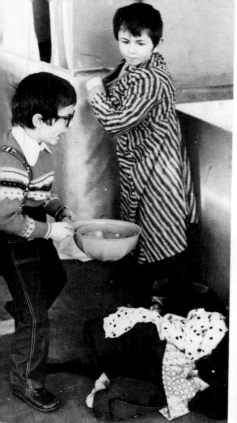

. . . and performing

Photo Camilla Jess

remember that this does not necessarily mean that you must put up forbidding-looking fences: careful siting of, for example, a catwalk for children to walk along can serve the dual purpose of blocking unwanted access. If you want to build an aerial runway – potentially one of the most exciting of structures, and one which can give an exceptional experience of movement even to children with extremely limited mobility if it is equipped with a secure chair or parachute harness – it should be one of the first items to site, normally down one side of the playground where other children will have no cause to cross its path.

The three basic elements of structures are slides, swings and opportunities for climbing; the three basic materials are wood, rope (or steel cable) and tyres. When starting to design them, try to look round other playgrounds for ideas: watch what the kids there are playing on the most, and ask their playworkers how their structures get used. Then think about your own ideas from a child's point of view: will the structures be *fun* to play on? Link them up, so there's more to do than simply climb up one side and down the other. Include things like tunnels and little cubbyholes that kids can treat as private spaces. Try to build a variety of challenges into the same structure, so that as children develop greater self-confidence or physical prowess they can progress from one to another. If, for example, you are building a slide, try to provide a number of ways of approaching it, of differing degrees of difficulty: a ramp, steps to another part of the structure, perhaps even a cargo net crossing over from another structure.

Try also to build structures that will encourage children to play together; this is particularly important with children with disabilities, whose experience of socialising with other children is often much more limited than that of able-bodied children. Slides should be large and wide, so that groups of children can go down them together. A good type of swing can be made by suspending a large tyre parallel to the ground, so that a whole lot of children can use it at once – which may mean that not a lot of actual swinging gets done, but ten or so children have a grand time climbing on and off it. (An extra advantage of this kind of swing is that, with a bean bag or large cushion placed on it, and some assistance from a worker or volunteer, it can be used by kids who have very limited mobility.)

Structures for a handicapped adventure playground are not as different from those on an ordinary playground as might be supposed, partly because many of the children using it are likely to be mentally handicapped, with few physical limitations, and, although it may take them longer to develop the necessary confidence, they need the same range of challenges as able-bodied children. What is really important is variety: play-workers should think about whether structures will offer some excitement to the whole range of children using the playground, from the most physically limited to the most able-bodied. It is not necessary for everything to be usable by all children, but it is essential that there should be adequate opportunities and challenges for every single child who uses the playground.

Wheelchair access is of course an important feature, but the vital point to bear in mind is that a playground needs to be designed for children, not for chairs: playground staff should be thinking about how to get kids out of their chairs and into the sand pit or the pond or on to the swings and the slides.

Children with disabilities have the same need for play as able-bodied children, and have a right to the same opportunities for exciting, adventurous experience. So don't think about designing structures for 'The Disabled': think about designing play structures for children, and then give detailed, careful thought to the minor design details which allow for those children's disabilities. Where you might have put a ladder, build steps, with deep treads so that children with problems of balance have plenty of room, and can if necessary go up on their backsides. Allow plenty of opportunities for climbing, but make the highest platform wheelchair accessible. Remember that the kids using a slide may not be able to correct their position easily, so make the sides high and padded. Provide an easy way down from high structures, so that a child's sense of achievement at having climbed up for the first time is not spoiled by worries about going down the same way when she suddenly realises how high she has come. And bear in mind that a lot of children with disabilities have problems of balance; this does not only apply to children with obvious mobility difficulties, but also to children with such conditions as blindness, deafness and Down's syndrome, all of whom may sometimes need a handrail to grip on to. Remember also that different disabilities cause different limitations: the ramp that aids the child in a wheelchair is an extra difficulty to the child who uses crutches.

One of the major differences between the children using a handicapped adventure playground and those to be found on an ordinary adventure playground is simply that their experience tends to be more limited. The feeling of freedom given by swings and slides may well be unfamiliar to both mentally and physically handicapped children, and is especially valuable for that reason. But this lack of experience may also cause a lack of self-confidence, of which playworkers need to be conscious. A blind child may need to go down a slide on a playworker's lap a few times before he develops the confidence to do it for himself.

Above all, never fall into the trap of becoming so concerned about the children's disabilities that you build structures that are very easy to get about – and thoroughly boring as a result. Structures are there to provide exciting activity, so don't design all the challenges out of them – think about how to help kids to meet those challenges. That's what an adventure playground is there for.

8 Adventure Play in Residential Settings

There is no need here to rehearse the arguments on the impact of institutionalisation on residents in long-stay mental handicap hospitals. We are now regularly exposed to reports and enquiries that have, quite rightly, taken place on the conditions that exist in these facilities. The more attention the better as far as we are concerned. The public at large needs to be confronted with the reality of long-term care for hospital residents, and indeed the pressures under which many of the staff who work in such settings find themselves. There is no doubt that this area has a low priority status in terms of allocation of resources and attractiveness of working conditions (Jay Report, 1979), and it will take a major effort to change this. It is not the purpose of this chapter to pursue this argument, but it is important to bear those issues in mind while looking at adventure play opportunities in residential settings. We would refer people to Maureen Oswin's book *The Empty Hours* (Allen Lane, 1971), which is relevant to our discussion of play and recreational opportunities for disabled children in hospitals.

Two other points need mentioning before we focus specifically on play facilities. Firstly, although we are here talking about long-stay hospitals, we must realise that we are also talking about people's places of residence, in some cases their only home. It is therefore important that we refer to people living in such communities as 'residents' and not 'patients'. A lot of people in long-stay hospitals have lived there for many years and perhaps have rare or fleeting contact with family or friends. For them, hospital is home, even if not an ideal one, and should be recognised as such.

Secondly, the age range of people living in long-stay hospitals is wide: there is a need for the whole population to have access to play and recreational activities, especially as, with greater emphasis being put on community care from the earliest days leading to a correspondingly lower number of children being admitted to hospital, the hospital population is now getting older. Play is not, and should not be, confined to children and adolescents. One of the present authors has a particularly happy memory of a visit to one hospital adventure playground where he saw a sixty-year-old man, smiling broadly, with trousers rolled up to his knees, playing with a bucket and spade in a sand pit.

Play facilities, in the form of activities on hospital wards, toy libraries and in-hospital schools, existed before any adventure playground was established, but it was a slow, often painful growth. In our opinion this was due to play activities being seen as rather disruptive to institutional routine, and also as a fairly nebulous, unhelpful activity by medical and management personnel.

With time, however, and the pioneering work of organisations such as the National Association for the Welfare of Children in Hospital (NAWCH) and Save the Children Fund, play in long-stay hospital settings became more accepted. One of the major turning points came with the appointment of part-time and full-time ward playworkers who actually operated from within the hospitals. The funding for these posts was, and often still is, precarious, but an important step had been taken.

From this beginning, individuals and organisations were able to promote play from within the hospital setting and work with residents, alongside medical staff. It would be wrong to assume, however, that this was a smooth process accepted by all. Indeed, a number of hospitals only resorted to appointing playworkers because of the pressure that was being put on them by successive reports on poor conditions and facilities for residents. It still remains true that, despite substantial progress, a lot of work needs to be done in securing play activities as an integral part of long-stay hospital life.

During 1981, the International Year of Disabled People, the Save the Children Fund came up with an original idea for promoting play of all types in mental handicap hospitals. They created a project called PLAYTRAC, consisting of a caravan which was taken around hospitals by two full-time workers. The caravan acted as a mobile play resource centre, with the two members of staff organising workshops and activities for residents and hospital personnel, both inside and outside the hospital wards. Unfortunately, the project had to close due to lack of funds in the summer of 1983. It had, however, started to make an impact by helping hospital staff, in particular, focus on play as an issue which was of importance to residents. Save the Children Fund have produced a report on PLAYTRAC's work, further details of which can be found in the reference section of this book.

Without the groundwork that organisations like Save the Children Fund carried out, and the slow conversion of some hospital staff, it is unlikely that fully-staffed adventure playgrounds would have got off the ground when they did. (The first, at St Lawrence's Hospital in Caterham, opened in 1974.) As we have seen in previous chapters, undertaking such a project is no simple task, and commitment to the concept is essential if it is to be seen to fruition.

Setting up a Hospital Playground

All the adventure playgrounds that have been established in hospitals have been initiated from within: medical, management or social service staff working at the hospital have provided the initial impetus and energy. In most cases, it has been the task of several individuals, who have promoted and fought for the creation of such a project, often against some apathy, always against lack of resources.

The first step is to get a group of people from a number of relevant disciplines who are interested in establishing a playground. Involving lay management and medical personnel is important here. If such people do not want to sit on a playground committee, make sure they at least support the concept of such a project, for they will have a large say in the location and funding of the project. It is also useful to include people from outside the hospital setting, such as special school teachers, parents and representatives from local play organisations. Once a core group has been brought together, real plans can start to be laid.

The group, or committee, as it must become if the project is to be successfully established, needs to discuss whether it will operate under the auspices of the hospital administration as a sub-committee, or whether it wants to become a separate charity capable of a degree of independence. Jonathan Page adventure playground at Manor House Hospital in Aylesbury is an example of a project which is an independent registered charity. St Lawrence's Hospital playground, on the other hand, operates without a charity number and is closely integrated into the hospital administration. The advantages and disadvantages of the two approaches can only really be assessed at local level.

It is crucial that, whatever its status, the committee has an understanding of the structure and nature of its own particular hospital and Health Authority. Issues ranging from funding to health and safety, management accountability to staff conditions, will differ from those applying to playgrounds run by local authorities and independent charities, and it is important to be fully aware of this.

From the very beginning the playground committee must 'sell' the project around the hospital so that its development is viewed as a positive addition to hospital facilities. This process will be helped if ward play staff already exist within the hospital, but can also be enhanced by organising workshops, talks and films. Visits to existing playgrounds can also be useful, and prove to the sceptics that such a project can be a success. As we have mentioned before in this book, the practicalities of establishing an adventure playground can take a long time, time which needs to be spent in promoting the idea to as many people as possible.

Having brought together a committee of interested people and proceeded to publicise the scheme, the next step is to identify a suitable site within the hospital grounds. The criteria for such a site are the same as those outlined in Chapter 3: good access, interesting landscape, suitable drainage and room for a sizeable playhut. With a site earmarked, or possibly a couple of alternative sites, attention needs to be turned to the funding of the project. This is where a knowledge of Health Service resources becomes important, as this would be the first line of enquiry. The two bodies to be approached via the hospital would be the local District and Regional Health Authorities. This is where the support of hospital management personnel in particular is important for a playground.

It is the experience of all the existing hospital adventure playgrounds that they could not survive on Health Service funding alone, and so from the outset the project committee needs to launch its own fund-raising activities. Local trusts, industry and commerce are obvious targets. A good relationship with the Friends of the Hospital can also be most valuable.

At St Lawrence's Hospital it was the League of Friends who were really the major force in establishing an adventure playground. They raised £20,000 towards the cost of the scheme, as well as providing numerous volunteers to clear and develop the site. They also provided half the costs of two members of staff, the other half being matched by the Croydon District Health Authority.

Exploring the possibility of some joint funding with the relevant local authority could also be helpful, particularly if children from outside the hospital will be using the playground. It is important to state here, as we have done elsewhere, that fund-raising is a major task in successfully establishing and running a hospital playground and that a lot of time and effort will have to be put into it.

With a committee established, publicity taking place and fund-raising in full swing, plans must be laid for the actual physical creation of the playground. A substantial playhut with good access, a cloakroom, kitchen, small office with a phone and adequate storage space are all crucial. Room for craft activities, sand and water toys, home-made wendy houses, games tables and soft play equipment will need to be considered. An open, light, airy hut is desirable, taking into account that hospital wards can often be dull and claustrophobic. A basic heating system is also necessary, particularly if the hut is to be used during winter months. We would recommend ducted hot air heating. As we have already discussed, the playhut must be sturdy and able to withstand considerable wear and tear, especially where floor surfaces are concerned.

Jonathan Page playground in Aylesbury has a prefabricated one-storey building as its play hut. This has not proved to be a very tough building and has had a number of problems: drainage from the flat roof; new floor covering; a flimsy internal skin. It is a tribute to the staff employed there that it has remained in almost constant use. St Lawrence's playground grew out of a restored cottage and two large adjoining barns which had to be restored, but which provide admirable indoor space for play activities (including a marvellous soft play room). Beckley adventure playground in Scott Hospital, Plymouth, initially ran its indoor activities from within the hospital school until it was able to afford a basic, sturdy wooden hut built at a cost of £4,500 with fixtures and fittings costing a further £9,000.

In addition to the building, the shape of the outside environment must be determined. Boundaries need to be defined and appropriate fencing considered. Fencing can be an expensive item to purchase: a lot of money can be saved if it is possible to take advantage of existing walls or fencing along one or more sides. Trees, bushes and grass with some undulating areas add to the character and atmosphere of a site and should be considered as an important part of it. A sand pit, pond, pathway, animal corner and areas for structure building need to be identified, as these are essential outdoor elements to the playground.

With both the play hut and outside area, the help and co-operation of the hospital Works Department is necessary. Planning staff from the District or Regional Health Authority may also need to be involved. This assistance is not just essential in the creation of the project, but also in its continued maintenance once open. The Authority experts can play an important role in designing the scheme and organising the practicalities of drainage, services (water, gas, electricity, phone), materials and costs. What they will need, however, is guidance about the nature of the project, so that plans are not so complex and grandiose that the sense of adventure play is lost. An adventure playground is not a Disneyland.

Once plans have been laid and money is coming in, building can start. Always be prepared to change plans up to the last minute – for example, re-designing the path because of shallow tree roots that are uncovered, or relocating the sand pit due to bad soil drainage on the original pit site.

Voluntary labour can be used for some of the basic tasks, or even, if there is some professional supervision, for some of the more complex work, such as erecting fence posts or digging out and laying a pond surface. The League of Friends or Hospital Voluntary Service Office can, and do, provide willing hands. The important point to remember, however, is that there should be one individual who is responsible for overseeing the physical development of the site, to whom people can turn for advice and guidance. That person should obviously be someone with appropriate technical skills, but also someone who is acceptable to both the project committee and the hospital authorities.

If there is enough money at this stage, we would recommend the early employment of a playworker. If skilled and mature enough, she could act as the site co-ordinator during development; if not, she could work alongside that person, organising volunteer labour, getting material, and of course promoting the project within the hospital and the wider community.

The Role of the Hospital Adventure Playworker

The employment of full-time playground workers is essential for the successful running of a project. We emphasise it here because we believe that you can not run an adventure playground, anywhere, without full-time staff. It is also important to employ this person as soon as possible. We would always recommend doing this well before the scheme is open to children, so that staff are familiar with the site, resources, management and potential users.

We have looked at the functions of playstaff in a previous chapter; the hospital playground worker has the same responsibilities, but there are some significant variations in how these should be implemented. The playground worker operating within the hospital setting needs to be familiar with the structure and nature of the hospital, and of the Health Service generally, both in terms of how things are organised, and of the dynamics that exist between separate professions in the field – as in the case of the relationship which exists between medical and administrative personnel. For a worker coming into the hospital environment from a local authority or charitable organisation it will take a little time to adapt to this new structure and her place within it.

It is important that the playground is seen as an essential part of hospital provision, and therefore project staff need to participate in the wider hospital life. They should see themselves, and be treated by other hospital personnel, as part of a multidisciplinary team working with the residents. They should, for example, take part in case conferences where information that has been picked up while a resident has been at the playground could be useful.

An original idea which is used at the Jonathan Page adventure playground is that of employing one of the three full-time members of staff to work half their hours on the playground and half on the hospital wards. While on the ward that worker can initiate play activities on the spot, with groups or individuals, or take people down to the playground itself. This way of working ensures that there is good, regular contact between the playground and the wards as well as a better understanding of the various needs of different residents.

Many staff in long-stay hospitals still view the residents they are working with from a medical perspective rather than a social one. Combined with poor staffing ratios and limited resources, this often produces rigidly methodical ways of working. This can grate with the staff from the adventure playground, who are trying to provide a free, exciting play facility which breaks away from conformity and strict order. It can, if staff are not careful, create a sense of isolation, where workers feel alienated from what exists in the rest of the hospital. If this problem is not confronted, constructive work on the project will be hindered.

It is obviously helpful to identify potential allies from the beginning, sympathetic people who will give the workers a lead into the system and possibly share similar frustrations.

Management Committee members would be an initial group to talk to, as well as people working in the hospital school, and its art, occupational and physiotherapy departments. These people are probably more flexible in their approach to residents than are many of the hospital staff, as well as being knowledgeable about various aspects of play.

The liaison worker idea employed at Jonathan Page is one way to overcome isolation, as is introducing play on to the hospital wards. Another way of informing staff about the playground's activities is to invite them down to the playground itself and get them involved in play activities. Ultimately, what we would like to see is play becoming an important part of the training curriculum for all medical staff.

It is our experience, and the experience of workers on adventure playgrounds in long-stay hospitals, that it can take considerable time to convince administrative and medical staff of the value of adventure play. Nevertheless, it is important to continue to press its claim hard and consistently even if the nature and structure of the hospital concerned do not meet with the approval of the play staff.

Voluntary help is important to all playground workers, and hospital projects are no different. The hospital Voluntary Services Officer is a good resource person here. There is also no reason at all why residents should not actually participate in voluntary work on the scheme. At several of the existing hospital playgrounds more able and mobile residents do help maintain the project (painting, tidying up), as well as running messages, making refreshments and playing with some of the visiting users. Do not forget this potential pool of workers.

One of the major roles of playground workers, in whatever setting, is to build links with hospital users and the local community. There is a danger of the staff working on a hospital project becoming enclosed within the hospital setting. This needs to be avoided. If schools or other groups from outside the hospital use the playground, isolation can be reduced, but it needs more than this. The workers should actively go out and participate in more community-based events, visit relevant schools and clubs, join the local or regional play association and generally promote the project outside the hospital. This often involves extra work over and above running and maintaining a playground, but we do feel it is an important function. It enables the workers to meet other people involved in play, and to see other forms of care experienced by people with disabilities in the community. It also opens up new areas for resources and support for the project, and puts the work of the hospital playground in a wider perspective.

Adventure Play and the Severely Handicapped

It is appropriate in this chapter to focus on the severely mentally and physically handicapped person who uses the adventure playground, as it is probably in hospitals that the highest concentration of such disabilities can be found. There are of course many severely disabled children living in the community, some of whom use, or could have access to, community-based adventure playgrounds: most of the comments here could equally well be applied to them.

We feel that all people, no matter how severe their disability, should be exposed to the adventure play environment, because such an environment should be so varied and stimulating that there has to be at least one activity in which an extremely disabled person can participate. It might be difficult and time-consuming to find one, but it can be done. An example will demonstrate how this works in practice.

Micky came regularly, twice a week, accompanied by an individual helper, to a playground in London. He was able to walk, but only in short, halting steps. He was very severely retarded, with no speech and only occasional grunts and screams. He was liable to self-mutilation and epileptic fits. If left on his own, he would stand and rock backwards and forwards.

For weeks staff struggled to find an activity that would stimulate him and elicit a smile. Eventually one was found. It was a swing on which Micky could lie as if he was in a bed; he was rocked slowly backwards and forwards on this swing bed with someone sitting beside him holding his hand, gently singing or talking to him. He would smile broadly and giggle. From this beginning, and the slow build-up of trust between the child and several workers, Micky graduated to climbing steps, going down slides and kicking and catching balls. It had been hard work, but once several activities which he enjoyed had been identified it produced a great feeling of success, which had repercussions elsewhere in his life. Thus, for example, he appeared more relaxed and better able to sleep while at home.

Mobility and movement are obvious problems for severely handicapped children in the adventure play setting. A great deal of help is consequently needed, to lift people on and off swings and structures, in and out of wheelchairs – plus, of course, pushing chairs. We would like to state very strongly here that staff, whether full-time or voluntary, must take great care while lifting and aiding people in this way. Numerous play workers have injured their backs through using incorrect methods, and many of these injuries have been long-term ones. We would recommend that workers seek advice from such people as physiotherapists about the right way to handle and lift these people.

Adequate staffing, full-time and voluntary, is one of the keys to working successfully with severely disabled people in the playground setting. A one-to-one ratio of staff to users is really necessary. If there is sufficient staffing every user should be found an activity.

It is possible not to have a constant one-to-one relationship if the playground is interesting and stimulating enough. For instance, having a group of people around a barbecue fire or an animal run while one or two members of staff co-ordinate a cooking activity or feeding of animals can be interesting and productive. One of the authors had a fascinating example of this shown to him on a hospital ward at Pedhill Hospital in Surrey, where one of the wards for the most severely handicapped adolescent boys was dominated by large tanks containing fish of all sizes, shapes and colours, plus coloured coral and plants. During quiet periods of the day the residents were put around these tanks to watch what was going on. The gurgles of satisfaction and interest were most apparent. As well as the fish tanks, bird cages containing parrots, budgerigars and assorted other birds were hung from the walls and ceilings! It was, in all, a most colourful, exciting atmosphere, to which the residents clearly responded.

It is our experience that simple ideas appeal most to severely mentally and physically handicapped people: kicking a ball, banging a tambourine, swinging movements, rolling on an inflatable or soft play material. For workers and volunteers these activities may sound too low-key and basic, but they illustrate the areas that need initially to be explored. Once an activity has been found that interests the individual person, it can be developed and experimented with. This process of identification and subsequent development is basic to adventure play.

It is with this group of people that the playground needs to consider the purchase of specialised equipment such as adapted chairs and mobile tricycles. It might not be necessary to buy these: they could be built on the playground or, as in the case of the St Lawrence's Hospital playground when it opened, by the hospital toymaker. The chapter on equipment looks at this in more depth.

We would hope anyway that the playground is full of spontaneous colour, sound, textures and smells which in themselves would produce a positive reaction in users. The very feeling of space can be important for people who have spent much of their lives in enclosed environments.

Finally, we would like to reiterate that it *is* possible for severely handicapped children and adults to use adventure play facilities, and that playstaff should not shirk working with this group. Indeed, they present a considerable challenge to the workers. Activities can and should be developed so that they can participate in the life of the playground, and staff should publicise that they can work with this difficult group.

Residential Homes

There are a large number of residential homes, as distinct from long-stay hospitals, in which disabled people live. Many have schools attached to them. Some of these residential units have large pieces of adjoining land, parts of which could be developed into adventure play areas. To develop a fully staffed playground would be beyond the resources of most of these facilities, although one boarding school run by the McIntyre Trust in Wingate, Buckinghamshire, developed an extremely successful project with one full-time leader, and operated it on an extremely low budget.

The point we should like to make here is that there is scope in many residential homes and schools for adventure play activities to take place – running a weekend playscheme, for example. There is little reason why small-scale adventure play projects should not flourish with part-time staff supervising and being responsible for the maintenance of equipment and site. A play hut may not be necessary, although storage space will be required for portable equipment such as bicycles and balls. Climbing frames, swings, outdoor water and sand play, a barbecue area and mobile equipment could make up some of the elements of such a project.

Obviously, some basic funding would be necessary to operate such a scheme. Resources might be available from the authority running the residential home or boarding school. Would they, for example, fund some part-time hours during the weekend or holiday periods? Contact with local play associations would also be useful in terms of getting equipment, raw materials and practical advice on how the scheme could operate. It is, in our view, important to utilise outdoor space as much as possible for the benefit of children and other residents, and not keep all of these areas neat, tidy and precise simply for the sake of show and order.

Fixed Play Equipment
By fixed play equipment we are here referring to manufactured products. These are looked at in more detail in Chapter 7; we mention them here because there are some specific criticisms that need to be made about how such equipment is sometimes used in residential institutions.

Over several years of visiting hospitals and residential homes the amount of old, decaying and dangerous manufactured play equipment that we have seen has been astonishing. There is nothing more dangerous in the field of children's recreation than young people playing on, or with, faulty equipment. In the past ten years Fair Play for Children has campaigned against the installation and purchase of poorly designed and built play structures, and highlighted the often appallingly poor maintenance of such items. Their work has concentrated on products which are to be found in public parks and open spaces, but there is no doubt that there is an abundance of such equipment in many hospital grounds.

Broken swing seats, concrete landing surfaces, steel posts rotting at ground level, jagged edges produced by weathering over the years, are all familiar features of poorly maintained sites. Not only this, but some of the equipment itself is often of a highly dangerous nature in its design, particularly if people with co-ordination, balance and perceptual problems are meant to be using it. 'Witches' hats' and roundabouts are two obvious examples. Indeed, many local authorities have banned these pieces of equipment from their parks because they are considered a risk to able-bodied children. Why, then, are they still in use in hospitals and residential homes?

The blame cannot be laid solely at the equipment manufacturers' feet, for in some cases that we have come across, pieces of equipment were put in place some twenty years ago and have hardly been maintained since. All play structures, whether hand-made or manufactured, *must* be regularly checked. It is wrong to assume that because a piece is purpose-built, made of steel, chain or well-preserved wood, it is automatically safe and maintenance-free. Hospital authorities need to look for and root out this equipment before serious accidents occur. In any case, older manufactured play products are far less exciting than many of the new ones now on the market. More modern pieces are often better designed and softer, with some manufacturers developing products which are specifically built with disabled children in mind.

We would sound a cautionary note here on the purchase of fixed play equipment. We recognise its value in public parks and open spaces, but we also recognise its expense, often running into several thousand pounds for larger pieces. How much better could this money be spent in the hospital or residential setting by employing part-time or full-time workers, who are infinitely more resourceful, imaginative and flexible than steel and wooden structures, and who can also relate to and communicate with children!

9 Integration

We must confess to being somewhat cynical about the subject of integration on playgrounds. Workers and committee members on handicapped adventure playgrounds are frequently asked why they do not allow local able-bodied children greater use of their facilities. Would it not be beneficial for the children using the playground to have contact with able-bodied children of their own age, the argument runs, and would such mixing not educate able-bodied children and encourage them to accept the disabled? We would indeed be sympathetic towards such arguments if they were to be used to support proposals that ordinary adventure playgrounds should do more to cater for the children with disabilities within their local community; it is all too common for traditional adventure playgrounds to be used by children who have a physically or mentally handicapped brother or sister whose very existence is not known to the playground's workers. But while provision for children with disabilities remains as scant as it is at present, we can see no justification for reducing what already exists in order to make room for children whose need for our playgrounds' facilities is much less than that of the children we would be forced to turn away.

Integration is not at present a practical option for most existing handicapped adventure playgrounds. Such playgrounds normally find that there is a very heavy demand for use of their facilities. They are forced to turn down schools and other organised groups who would like to use the playground, or to limit the frequency of their visits, and lack the resources to cater for other areas of need that are apparent to them. This situation arises not so much from a lack of funding for individual playgrounds – although that is an undoubted difficulty for many projects – as from a more general lack of provision. At the time of writing, Britain has less than twenty adventure playgrounds for handicapped children, most of which, with the exception of the eight London playgrounds, each provide the only such facility within a very large area. There are two in the North of England – both on Merseyside – one in Plymouth and one in Glasgow, which is as yet the only such playground in the whole of Scotland. And when children with disabilities do not have access to one of these playgrounds, it is unlikely that there will be many alternative facilities that can provide them with equivalent opportunities. In such circumstances, playgrounds become understandably reluctant to adopt any course of action which restricts the number of children with disabilities for whom they can cater. We very much hope that a day will come when we shall see playgrounds that exist to serve all the children of their local community, whatever their disability or lack of it, but the realisation of that dream is some way off as things stand at present. If it is to be brought to reality in the foreseeable future, that can not be done by the handicapped adventure play movement in isolation, but requires a considerable change of attitude by the traditional adventure playgrounds, most of which are currently guilty of unconscious discrimination against an important section of their local community. (There are, however, honourable exceptions; for example, Stamshaw Park, a recently-opened adventure playground in Portsmouth, provides facilities for children with disabilities, and is developing this aspect of its work on the principle that such children need to be integrated with the normal work of the playground rather than form a separate area of work. This playground is described in issue 37 of *Play Times*.)

The argument for integration is in any case based on a misunderstanding of the nature of adventure playgrounds for handicapped children. Though we can see definite advantages to the prospect of such playgrounds being based on a smaller catchment area, more nearly resembling that of a conventional adventure playground, we do not feel that the children currently using these playgrounds are missing out on anything of great importance by not sharing them with larger numbers of able-bodied children. We also feel that the non-integrated approach is not without certain advantages of its own.

What is frequently forgotten is that children with disabilities do not constitute a single, neatly-classifiable group, with a single set of characteristics and abilities. The children who use existing handicapped adventure playgrounds cover the entire spectrum of physical, mental, sensory and emotional disability. It is possible, on existing playgrounds, to see blind children playing with sighted, deaf children playing with hearing (and communicating perfectly adequately while they do so), mentally handicapped children playing with others of normal intelligence, children in wheelchairs being pushed about by more mobile friends. If those friends have disabilities of their own, what does it matter? The friendship is what is really important. In any case, playgrounds that avoid large-scale integration do normally deliberately cater for some able-bodied kids: brothers and sisters of children using the playground, a personal friend who has been brought along or the children of playworkers or committee members. As a lot of the children who use these playgrounds have disabilities which are not immediately visible, the question of who is or is not able-bodied is often, in practice, not a very significant one: children's personalities are a much more important factor than their disabilities.

It is often possible to let local able-bodied children use the playground at certain times. For this to happen, a clearly thought-out policy needs to be laid down, and explained to the children. Such a policy should specify when they are allowed on the playground, how many able-bodied children are allowed on at any one time, and that they must be aware of the needs of the disabled children using the project.

Some children who use handicapped adventure playgrounds would not fare at all well on conventional adventure playgrounds. This is partly a matter of specialised facilities, such as wheelchair access. Obviously some more severely disabled children would be likely to get left out of many of the activities of any playground that was geared primarily to able-bodied children. But there is also a large group of children for whom the problem is primarily a psychological one: a lack of self-confidence, shyness and inexperience at socialising with others of their own age, even a lack of experience of how to play (because play is in many ways a learnt activity). For these children, a non-integrated playground can act as a stepping stone to the larger world, somewhere to face challenges at their own pace, acquire self-confidence and physical skills. Eventually, when they are ready, they'll do their own integrating in the outside world, perhaps even on other adventure playgrounds, but in the meantime they need somewhere that is geared to their particular needs. Many such children, for example, would find it very difficult to cope with a completely unstructured play environment.

The specialist skills of the experienced playworker are of great importance in this respect. Some children with disabilities are less self-assertive than their more able counterparts, less likely to demand to do a particular activity or to dragoon a playworker into helping them. Others, by contrast, are over-dependent on adult support. This places an extra responsibility on play-workers, who have to get to know the children using their playground, and learn to anticipate their needs to a greater extent than would be required on a conventional adventure playground. They need to know how to recognise when to leave children to play on their own, and when to step in and give the little bit of support that will boost a child's self-confidence – going down a slide, for example, with a child who hasn't quite plucked up the courage to do it on his own. They need to be able to adjust to the slower intellectual pace of educationally sub-normal children, who may need to be given the same explanation several times over before they get the hang of it. They also have to make some very tricky decisions of a sort which are unlikely to face workers on conventional adventure playgrounds: how much apparently anti-social behaviour should they be prepared to put up with, for example, from a child whom they know to be taking drugs which have the side-effect of tending to make her irritable?

Lady Allen commented, in *Adventure Playgrounds for Handicapped Children*, that 'Non-handicapped brothers, sisters and friends, in a ratio of about one-third able to two-thirds disabled children are welcome at the playground and help to create fuller, happier and more active sessions.' We agree with that statement, but wish to make some additional observations of our own. One third non-disabled children should be regarded as a maximum ratio, not necessarily as an ideal to be aimed for. Above that figure, a change starts to come over the playground, as its activities become dominated by the more able children: the Down's Syndrome child who's been having a good time knocking balls around the pool table finds his presence resented by children who want to play a 'proper' game, according to the rules; a child with poor balance starts worrying about getting knocked over; playworkers have to start worrying about whether the demands being made on them by more self-assertive children are distracting their attention from less able children who actually need it more.

It should also be realised that there is a considerable difference between a handicapped adventure playground that admits a certain number of able-bodied children and a playground that is 'integrated' in the sense referred to earlier. In the first place, it would not be possible, on an integrated playground, to control the ratio of able to disabled children; if a project exists for able-bodied children as much as for children with disabilities, they must be free, within its opening hours, to use it whenever they wish. That would almost certainly mean that able-bodied children would tend to outnumber children with disabilities by a fairly substantial margin. Allowing able-bodied children to use a handicapped adventure playground is a feasible measure partly because those children know that they are allowed in on the understanding that they recognise the needs of the children with disabilities using the playground. We should, in fairness, point out that many of the able-bodied children who do use handicapped adventure playgrounds, and perhaps particularly those who have a brother or sister who has a disability, are very good at working within these constraints, and pay a lot of attention to the individual needs of other children using the playground. But we have also come across cases of siblings who have evident emotional problems of their own related to their brother or sister's disability; the extent to which a playground sees dealing with such problems as part of its responsibility is a tricky decision, with no overall general solution: the playground staff must make their own decision about each individual case.

A further distinction, and one that is likely to cause particular difficulty to workers on conventional adventure playgrounds who are trying to find ways of making their facilities open to children with disabilities in their local community, is to be found in the fact that handicapped adventure playgrounds do not operate according to the basic assumption that children are free to come and go as they wish, without interference from the playground staff. There are good reasons for this: some of the children who use such playgrounds, such as autistic children, can not safely be allowed to go wandering about the streets, and are only brought to a handicapped adventure playground because their parents feel that they can leave them there without the need to fear that they might slip off on their own. We doubt whether most conventional adventure playgrounds would be willing to introduce the sort of safeguards that would make it possible for such children to use their facilities, and are not at all sure that it would be desirable for them to do so: the principle of free access on which such playgrounds normally work is an important one, and worth preserving. This does seem to imply that there are certain children who could not be integrated into conventional adventure playgrounds, or conversely, that able-bodied children could not be fully integrated into handicapped adventure playgrounds without the abandonment of some important principles of the adventure playground movement. But there are undoubtedly many children with disabilities who could well use conventional adventure playgrounds with a minimum of inconvenience: in a lot of cases, all that would be needed would be to let parents know that their children would be welcome. We can not say precisely where the line should be drawn; that is something that will differ from playground to playground and can only be worked out in practice. That will happen once conventional adventure playgrounds accept their responsibility to the children with disabilities within their local community, and start trying to tackle the problem that, at present, most of them do not even recognise. We predict that, once they do so, workers on these playgrounds will find the task less difficult than they might assume: they may have little experience of disability, but the major skills that would be needed would be the basic skills of working with children they already possess. Certainly, we in the handicapped adventure play movement will be delighted to offer support and ideas to any playground that wishes to make the attempt.

For the reasons given above, we do not feel that new handicapped adventure playgrounds should be set up as fully-integrated schemes. Nevertheless, there are certain circumstances in which integration is the appropriate solution. One, obviously, occurs when an existing conventional playground or holiday scheme starts to cater for children with disabilities. Thus, in the early 1970s Blacon adventure playground in Chester ran for several years a successful scheme whereby part of their site was set up so that it could be used by children with disabilities. This scheme came to an end when the playworker who had initiated it left the playground: if integration is to work successfully in the long term, there must be a strong commitment to it from playground staff and management.

In some cases, integrated play may be the most appropriate choice for purely practical reasons. In particular, when the initial impetus for a project comes from a group of parents of children with disabilities, concerned at the lack of facilities for their children, they are likely to want rapid results, and may therefore favour the possibility of persuading an existing playground or playscheme to start operating as an integrated project. Alternatively, if another group of parents is campaigning about a more general lack of provision for all children in the area, the two groups may find it convenient to unite their resources and press for an integrated scheme.

A third reason for setting up an integrated playground or playscheme occurs when the project develops from a smaller scheme, such as a PHAB (Physically Handicapped/Able Bodied) Club, which is itself integrated. (PHAB is a national network of integrated youth clubs, which work on the premise that, while ordinary youth clubs may not cater adequately for young people with disabilities, clubs that are established specifically for 'the handicapped' are liable to prove over-protective.) This was what happened with the most successful example of integrated play that has come to our attention, the Sheffield Children's Integrated Play Association (SKIP), where a single experimental integrated playscheme has grown into a charity that in 1983 ran three playschemes, and supported another three and several integrated youth clubs.

SKIP started in 1975, with what was described as a 'PHAB playscheme' in Sheffield's Greenhill Park and Greenhill/Bradway Youth Centre, integrating physically disabled and able-bodied young people. The scheme was a success, though a report by its leader, Lois Burke, drew attention to the need for more detailed advance planning for future projects, in the areas of budgeting, definition of staff roles, timing of programme and transport, provision of information to parents and holding staff meetings. The report drew particularly firm attention to the need for an adequate complement of capable full-time helpers, commenting that, 'voluntary helpers should, preferably, be involved at the planning stage'. A more ambitious playscheme was organised for the following year. Also in 1976, interested adults from the statutory and voluntary sectors first met formally as SKIP, 'to promote the philosophy of making existing play provision accessible to disabled children and young people'.

In 1977, its third year of operation, SKIP expanded its activities, and held two summer schemes, one at Greenhill/Bradway, and a second at Meynell Youth Centre. During that year, SKIP extended its membership and formally elected officers prior to seeking charitable status. When Greenhill/Bradway began a weekly integrated club evening, friendships started on the summer playscheme were enabled to continue on throughout the year. In 1978, a third scheme, at Hurlfield Youth Centre, was added to the first two, and the Sheffield Children's Integrated Play Association was formally constituted and launched at a public meeting in November; it was granted charitable status the following year. The appointment of a temporary full-time worker in 1979, with funding from the Manpower Services Commission, enabled the organisation to operate with greater efficiency and undertake further initiatives.

The Greenhill/Bradway Youth Centre extended its integrated club evenings to three nights a week.

SKIP's three regular summer playschemes, all of which have now been running for at least five years, attract children from all over Sheffield. Children with disabilities form between 10 and 40 per cent of the total number of children using the scheme; these have generally been fairly severely disabled children, most of whom are wheelchair users. Though all three schemes have recently started to include a number of mentally handicapped children, it is fair to say that SKIP has to date tended to cater for children with a substantially narrower range of disabilities than is the norm within the handicapped adventure play movement. All three playschemes have tended to have a much less satisfactory response to invitations sent out via local special schools than they would have liked, and SKIP have come to the conclusion that it may be necessary to establish personal contact with the parents of potential users. This difficulty seems to be related to the infrequency of annual schemes, since, where weekly integrated clubs linked to the summer schemes have been established, there has been a considerably higher attendance of children with disabilities at the summer playschemes.

One of the most impressive results of SKIP's activities has been the establishment of three smaller community-based independent summer playschemes. Run entirely by local parents, these three schemes have received the bulk of their funding from the city's Recreation Department; though they have received support from SKIP, this has not included any financial assistance. Though smaller in size, these schemes have tended to have a higher proportion of children with disabilities, probably because they have been more geared to locating them, and have established a closer personal contact with parents. Members of the group initially visit the parents of local children with disabilities in their own homes, to explain how the schemes work, answer any questions the parents may have and check on their child's personal requirements. This has proved to be a very successful method of recruitment: over 90 per cent of parents thus approached agree to their children attending a playscheme. (Obviously, it would not be easy to put such an approach into practice when planning a larger scheme, with many more families to be visited, over a much larger catchment area. In view of its obvious success, however, this might well be a valuable method for a conventional adventure playground that has decided it wishes to involve a greater number of children with disabilities from its local community: initial approaches to parents could be made through local special schools, existing disability organisations or the local social services department.)

SKIP's activities appear to be bringing about a substantial change in attitudes to disability within the local community. More than a dozen existing local playschemes and youth clubs have expressed an interest in turning themselves into integrated projects. This is obviously a very heartening development, but brings a new set of problems to be faced. SKIP have learnt that it is more difficult to integrate an existing scheme than to start a community-based scheme that is integrated from the very beginning, and that younger children tend to integrate more easily than older ones; one response to this has been to establish integrated junior clubs for younger children.

The direction of SKIP's current development appears to be towards encouraging existing projects to integrate, promoting junior clubs and supporting the setting-up of playschemes that have a stronger community base than SKIP's original large schemes. This approach clearly has a strong relevance to the current interest in ideas of community care for children with disabilities. As such, it faces a familiar problem: whether SKIP is able to continue its impressive record of success is a question that is liable to depend on the availability or otherwise of adequate funding from statutory bodies. As SKIP is already demonstrating, community-based projects can be a highly effective way of using such funding; they can not, however, be an alternative to it. The success of community-based projects remains strongly linked to the degree of commitment shown by sources of statutory funding. We hope that SKIP continues to receive the degree of financial support that its remarkable achievements to date indicate that it deserves.

An interesting example of another approach to provision of integrated play facilities is provided by the integrated play park in Ward End Park, Birmingham. This project, undertaken by the NPFA in co-operation with industry and local government to commemorate the International Year of Disabled People, was conceived as 'a traditional playground designed specifically to enable *all* children, including disabled, to play together'. The playground was based on an existing site, which already contained some play equipment and a permanent play centre with full-time play leaders. The extension of these facilities was planned in consultation with specialist agencies such as PHAB and the RNIB, with local requirements being assessed by consultation with potential user groups such as special schools. Finance for the alterations came from the Coca Cola Export Corporation, who undertook to provide the £50,000 cost, donating half of it themselves and raising the other half from other industrial sources and charitable trusts. A detailed description of this project can be found in issue 34 of *Play Times*.

What we would ideally like to see would be a two-tier system of provision of adventure play facilities. One tier would consist of integrated playgrounds, such as could be established if existing conventional adventure playgrounds were to start catering for the needs of children with disabilities. The second would consist of handicapped adventure playgrounds with more limited integration, such as already exist; these would work primarily with the most severely disabled children, for whom other playgrounds might be unable to cater adequately, and children who had not yet acquired enough self-confidence to hold their own among able-bodied children in their local community adventure playground. We would not see any place for playgrounds that did not cater for children with disabilities at all: although such discrimination is probably largely unconscious and unintended, we see it as essentially contradictory to the basic ideals of the adventure playground movement. As this is a statement of an ideal situation, rather than one which is likely to be immediately realised, we would also stipulate that these two types of playground would form a network that covered the entire country. We do not expect to see this dream fully realised within the foreseeable future. We would however point out that it is by no means an impractical fantasy. If the will existed to create legislation that would entitle children to adequate provision of play facilities, and to provide adequate funding for the purpose, it would be perfectly practicable to create such a system. Even without the legislative support, we can be working towards such an ideal. All it takes is determination.

10 Playschemes and Holiday Projects

Although this book is primarily about adventure playgrounds, we do not want to neglect the work that is done on holiday and weekend playschemes, many of which have an adventure play element to them. Several hundred playschemes take place in Britain every year and provide, particularly during holiday periods, an important and valued service to children. We feel that the playscheme movement is one of the largest, most direct and available grassroots services available to children and families, and often carries out much positive and progressive work with them. It is time that local authorities and professional workers, teachers, social workers and health workers, among others, realised the importance of playschemes and stopped treating them merely as a way of keeping children off the streets.

Holiday and weekend playschemes frequently act as the starting point for more permanent provision. Chelsea Adventure Playground and the Thames Valley Handicapped Adventure Playground Association both grew out of holiday playschemes. It might not be feasible for people interested in starting a full-time playground to get it going quickly, because of lack of finances or unavailability of a suitable site, but the development of a playscheme might present a viable alternative which has, as its long term aim, the creation of a full-time project.

Anyone thinking of organising such a playscheme will find it worth getting hold of such information packs and booklets as the NPFA's *How to Organise a Holiday Playscheme* and SKIP's *Integrating Disabled Children in Play*, details of which are given in the reference section of this book. Most local or regional play associations are heavily involved in organising and co-ordinating playscheme activities, and would be more than willing to offer advice and support. Other sections of this book, such as the equipment and resources chapters, are also relevant to playschemes.

As with a playground, the first task is to research the need for a playscheme and gather support. This involves visiting special schools, special needs clubs, social services, health services and individual families. From this it will be possible to gauge whether there is a genuine demand for such provision. If starting absolutely from scratch it will be necessary to call a gathering of all interested parties, either in the form of a public meeting or of inviting representatives to a more private session. We would recommend the former, as an approach that will encourage a wide range of participants and potentially more support.

If there is an existing play association in your area, like the Merseyside Play Action Council or Glasgow Playschemes Association, they need to be contacted as soon as possible. Such bodies will help to organise meetings and provide information from the early stages of planning onwards. One of the first moves of a new group wishing to start a playscheme for children with disabilities should be to affiliate to any existing play organisations in the area. This immediately puts them in contact with existing bodies of knowledge and expertise which will make the task of creating a playscheme that much easier.

From a meeting of people who have shown an interest it is useful to form a core group, or committee, which can then start to lay down plans for the project. Such a group should have a broad representation of people and organisations on it, and be made up of individuals who are prepared to share what at times can be a considerable workload, especially during the period leading up to the opening of the scheme. Apart from the more traditional committee posts of Chairperson, Secretary and Treasurer, it is also useful to have at least one person who will act as Resource and Materials Co-ordinator, and make it her job to gather equipment and other items necessary for the successful running of the playscheme.

The committee's first responsibility will be to find suitable premises for the project. Issues that need to be borne in mind include having a building, or space within one, that is at one level, or if this is not possible making sure that there is easy access to a higher floor by lifts or ramps. Even if the premises are all on one level, there need to be as few steps as possible at, for instance, the entrance and exit points. There must be good toilet, washing and changing facilities, and easy access to a telephone in case of accidents or other emergencies. Doors need to be wide enough to take wheelchairs, and there must be adequate parking space outside so that minibuses, cars and perhaps even coaches can pull up and let the children out on to the site. Other considerations concern the space available, both indoors and outdoors, where numerous activities will take place and equipment will have to be properly stored. Playscheme activities can be noisy, colourful and adventurous, and so it is important to know that any facility you might obtain can be used in such a way, given the consequent possibility of a broken window or paint being dropped on the floor, for example. We have come across schemes which have found out after a few days of operating that there are so many restrictions placed upon them that many of their activities become meaningless and boring. Check out at an early stage the extent to which the facility can be used.

Places to approach for possible use include schools, which are usually empty during holiday or weekend periods, community and youth centres, church halls, existing adventure playgrounds and local parks, where there may be pavilions from which a project could operate. Start by contacting the people who work on the premises. If they are willing to support you, it is quite likely that an approach for permission will have to be made to the relevant local authority department – which will usually be Recreation, Education or Housing. If the facility is privately run, you will need to approach its own management committee. We know of playschemes that have operated from all of the above types of facility, although it is in our experience most common for such projects to be based at local authority special schools.

Once suitable premises have been found, the committee has to start to decide the nature and structure of the playscheme. How many children can it take? Should they be of mixed disabilities? What catchment area should the scheme serve? For how many weeks should it run, and how many hours a day should it be open? Should there be an age limit? If it is an integrated project, should there be a set ratio of able-bodied children to children with disabilities? All these questions need to be answered at an early stage. It is probable that when premises have been found some of the above questions, such as opening times and numbers, will automatically be answered. Some of the other issues may be more difficult to solve, as with the questions of integration or mixed disabilities. It is worth taking a little time to clarify these so that the project can go ahead with a clear policy in mind. On the issue of integration, we advise readers to consult Sheffield Children's Integrated Play Association for ideas. For a fuller discussion of their work, see Chapter 9.

Other issues, such as catchment areas, have to be discussed locally and depend on the resources available to a scheme – money and transport in particular. We would advise schemes that are just starting not to plan on a grand scale. Build a playscheme up in a way with which you know you can cope, and within the resources available. Even if this means operating with just 10–12 children it is worth it. If the scheme is a success numbers can be increased at the next holiday period, and so gradually built up. Success on whatever scale breeds confidence and respect from others, and gives a group strength to develop its work. It is better, in our opinion, to go about it in this way, and make mistakes on a limited level, than to have major failures of a sort that prove expensive both financially and emotionally.

As soon as a basic structure has been thrashed out and premises found, money has to be raised to finance the project. As with full-time adventure playgrounds, this divides into three areas: local authority funding; support from commerce, industry and charitable trusts; and a group's own fund-raising efforts. A fuller discussion of fund-raising is given in Chapter 6, but some extra points need to be made here.

Many local authorities do have money available for play-schemes, particularly during summer holiday periods. The money can be distributed in a number of ways. The two most common are direct grant-giving to individual projects, and giving the total amount budgeted for to an umbrella body, such as a local play association, which then distributes that amount between its members or affiliates. Most of this money will come via the Recreation and Leisure departments.

Whatever way it is distributed, an application will have to be made in writing to the local authority or relevant play organisation. To find out more about how to go about this, contact the play or recreation officer in the local authority, or the secretary or play co-ordinator working with the local play association. Money for special needs schemes may also be available through the Education Department or the District Health Authority; contact the local Education Officer or Community Health Council as appropriate. There may also be the chance of joint funding from the local authority and health authority combined. Again, contact the Community Health Council or District Health Authority and the local Social Services Department for advice. Gaining support from such statutory services as Community Mental Handicap Teams, as Cleveland Playschemes for Handicapped Children does, will also help in fund-raising efforts, as well as providing valuable advice and facilities, potential users and other resources such as, in particular, equipment and transport.

Some playschemes are run by local authority services. Walsall's Education Department, for instance, runs playschemes for children with disabilities. In such cases, funding comes straight to the department and into a local authority service. There is then direct administration and management from a statutory source. For voluntary groups fund-raising is more complex. They may have to decide whether to become an independent registered charity so that they can fund-raise freely, and accept grants and donations, or affiliate to another body and raise money under their umbrella. One of these options must be considered so that the group can take money in to run the playscheme. If a committee is not either registered as a charity or affiliated to one it will find raising funds more difficult, as many organisations and individuals will simply not give grants or donations to non-charitable bodies. However tiresome this procedure of registering or affiliating might be, we strongly urge groups to do it.

Extra money is often available to full-time projects during holiday periods. The assumption made by some authorities is that during the summer months in particular children need more play and recreational provision; so they make extra money available to existing adventure playgrounds in order that they can expand their activities and staffing to meet the extra demands placed upon them. It is therefore worthwhile for projects to approach their local authority to see if such help is available. If it is not, pressure ought to be put on statutory services to provide extra resources for full-time schemes.

It is also essential to plan staffing for the playscheme; this can determine whether the scheme is successful or not. Enthusiastic and energetic workers full of ideas and originality will make a scheme hum and bubble. Badly motivated and lifeless workers will have the opposite effect. Staffing requirements will depend on the number of children attending and the tasks that need to be carried out to make a scheme successful, such as organising drivers and escorts for transport, and arranging day trips or visits to swimming baths and other places of interest. Such staffing estimates will need to be put in any grant application, because staffing costs will be the most expensive item of the playscheme's budget. How to pay staff, and at what rate, has to be a local decision based on the money that is available to the project.

There needs to be a playleader or co-ordinator; ideally, this person ought to be someone who has experience of running a playscheme and also has some knowledge of disability. There also needs to be a team of playstaff who plan the activities and programme in conjunction with the co-ordinator. This process should involve the management group, who will have been planning the project for many months before staff arrive. Among the workers there needs to be at least one person who is skilled in first aid, and can deal with distributing medication to children and be familiar with other medical aspects of disability, such as how to cope with epileptic fits, helping children who have bad asthmatic attacks or dealing with pressure sores on children who have physical handicaps.

It is also useful for several of the staff to be able to drive. This applies both to cars and minibuses. Access to transport is crucial to a project's success, as we shall see later in this chapter.

We strongly recommend that playscheme staff have at least one day's training or induction before they start work. This would not just concentrate on disability issues but cover a whole range of subjects ranging from how to lift children to fire alarm procedures, from how to make toys from scrap to arranging outings and trips. If there are a number of playschemes operating in one area it would be advisable to plan joint training schemes, as already happens in many areas. Such training should be budgeted for from the beginning.

A scheme needs to advertise for staff, although, if it has been going for several years and has built up a good reputation workers will often come back for more! Besides contacting the local press to help with advertising, it is also worth approaching local colleges, voluntary workers' bureaux and youth and community centres. Organisations like Quaker Work Camps and International Voluntary Service (IVS) will also help, and often provide staff at little or no cost to the playscheme, as well as offering an international flavour to proceedings. Do not, however, forget the most local resource of all in terms of staff, namely local people and parents. Rather than alienate them from the work of the playscheme, involve them as much as possible.

Ideally, the playleader should be employed several weeks before the project opens so that she can, with the committee, prepare the administration side of things, although by this time children should have been informed of the basic details of the scheme, such as venue, times and possible costs. This is important to bear in mind, as many families who have a child with a disability need to plan a long way ahead because of other commitments such as hospital appointments or family holiday arrangements. This contacting of children should be helped by having people on the management group who are in direct contact with children and their families, such as social workers or parents. Otherwise, notices should be sent out via special schools and other special needs organisations such as Contact a Family or MENCAP groups. SKIP's experience does, however, indicate that a more direct approach to individual families gets much better results: see Chapter 9.

Other administrative points that need to be sorted out include the creation of a register of children who will be attending. This can be done by sending returnable slips to parents so that they can indicate when their child will be coming. It does not have to be a rigid system and names can be continually added even as the project is running. It is useful, however, to know who is coming and when, so that transport in particular can be satisfactorily arranged, and people who want to come do not get left behind because no one knew they wanted to come. On forms that indicate what days a child might attend it is also useful to ask for basic details about the child's disability, any medication he may be having and who should be contacted in case of emergency. Parental consent forms are also necessary if children are to be taken on trips. Again, these do not all have to be in at the beginning of the scheme, so long as they are available when a trip is made. It should be the responsibility of the playleader, in conjunction with the committee secretary, or local authority officer if it is a statutory-run scheme, to keep this information in order, and to hand, in case it is needed at short notice.

Another major administrative responsibility is insurance, which should be organised well before the scheme starts. Public liability insurance is necessary to protect the playscheme against possible legal action. This may need to be extended to protect the interests of the leaseholders or local authority on whose premises the playscheme is operating. Equipment insurance is also advisable, as it is quite likely that damage due to vandalism, accidents or hard use may occur. Personal accident insurance for staff should also be considered, and it is necessary to check that all vehicles used by the scheme are adequately insured. Failure to have good insurance cover is a very serious matter, and a playscheme should simply not open without it. Information on insurance can be got from the local play association or local authority Recreation Department, both of whom may operate a policy under which any new scheme could come.

Once a playscheme is running, other administrative details need to be taken care of. It will be necessary to keep an accident book in which to record injuries to staff and children. An incident book in which breakages are recorded is also important, especially if the scheme is based in a school and school property is damaged. Health and Safety regulations are just as important in this sphere as they are on adventure playgrounds. The daily flow of money also needs to be maintained. A project will need a constant flow of cash with which to buy materials as well as requiring money from children for day trips or visits to swimming baths or zoos.

When the playscheme is running, all the staff on it should be aware of the administrative procedures that operate on it. The playleader/co-ordinator may be the one who planned the structure in the weeks leading up to the project's opening, but it is very important that she inform everybody about how it works. Confusion and some anger can be caused by people not understanding, or not being familiar with, the administrative base of the scheme. This can lead to money not being properly accounted for or accidents not being properly recorded and a scheme being considerably weakened as a result.

Transport is the next issue to consider. There is no use planning a playscheme unless people have considered how children will get there. Many children with disabilities can not use public transport, and some can not make their own way to a scheme because of the severity of their handicap; they therefore rely on transport being provided. Parents can of course bring children if they have a car. It is often worth finding out whether such parents would be prepared to pick up other children on their way to the project. The other alternatives are to approach the local authority social service or education departments to see if they will help, or to contact other voluntary organisations in the area, such as the Red Cross or PHAB.

During holiday periods education authority transport is often not used, and so might be available to playschemes. A valuable feature of such transport is that it is often adapted with tail-lifts so that wheelchairs can be taken on and off. These vehicles will have to be driven by local authority coach drivers but projects will usually have to provide escorts to supervise picking the children up. The disadvantage of transport belonging to other organisations, whether statutory or voluntary, is that they may well want to use their buses at the same time as you do. It is best, therefore, to approach these people as long as possible before a scheme starts.

If there are a number of playschemes in the same area or a co-ordinating play association, it may well be the case that a transport pool can be created which could help a project working with children with disabilities. Remember, though, that a playscheme working with special needs children will need transport every day and not just on selected occasions. So plan transport needs ranging from finance to personpower well ahead of the opening date. Experience has demonstrated again and again that a well thought-out transport programme enormously enhances the service a project offers and saves many frustrating hours while the scheme is in operation.

Adequately equipping a playscheme is, obviously, crucial to its successful running. Many of the materials and items found on an adventure playground can equally be used on a playscheme, although the more temporary nature of a holiday or weekend project does mean that large pieces of fixed outdoor equipment are less likely to be practicable. Another problem for play-schemes is that they tend not to own their own premises, which usually makes it more difficult to experiment with materials and equipment – for example, by painting windows and walls or building an indoor play structure.

Getting hold of a range of go-karts and bicycles, some of which should be adapted for use by physically handicapped children, is important. If a project can afford to buy several pieces of mobile equipment all the better; if not, a school or existing special needs club may be prepared to loan some – on condition that if they get broken they will be repaired or replaced! They may also be prepared to loan other aids and equipment on the same basis. Other outdoor equipment and activities should include water play provision, such as a large portable pool, a sand pit contained within a manufactured sand drum, an inflatable (which it may be possible to hire by the day), barbecue areas and space for games of all descriptions ranging from sports activities to informal ball or drama games.

The main focus of most playschemes' indoor activities is art and craft, although there is no reason why much of this should not take place outside, particularly if the weather is fine. Modelling, painting, pin-hole cameras, mask-making, printing and puppetry are just some of the things that can be done. To carry out these activities successfully, plenty of craft material is necessary, much of which can be recycled scrap. This is where the committee resources person mentioned earlier really comes into her own, for to have enough equipment to see a scheme through a big summer holiday period, collecting and scrounging needs to start early on. There is nothing more frustrating for a playscheme than running out of materials halfway through its intended time. Make sure you have planned this collection process carefully.

The inside will also be heavily used on rainy days, so there needs to be space and equipment for games to take place indoors. A wet day can cause chaos inside a building if activities are not carefully thought out, particularly if some of the children attending the project need relatively close attention or help, as a disturbed autistic child would, for instance. On days like this the workers are often stretched to their limit, both in terms of ideas and of patience. Good planning will help reduce this problem.

For further activities we refer readers to playscheme publications, which between them contain hundreds of different ideas for use in all kinds of projects, and in all types of weather.

Besides indoor and outdoor play equipment, it will be necessary to purchase such 'service items' as orange juice, toilet rolls, soap, coffee, first aid equipment and incontinence pads. The owners of the premises on which a project is based may well be prepared to let the playscheme use their goods on the condition that they are replaced when the scheme is finished. However this is organised, it is important to budget for these materials, as they contribute as much towards the smooth running of a scheme as the play equipment itself. (For a more detailed discussion of equipment, see Chapter 7.)

As on a playground, the playscheme site should be ready for use when children arrive in the morning, and cleared, cleaned and secured at the end of the day. It is always useful to strike up a good relationship with the caretaker of the building from which the project is operating. This can help enormously with the appropriate storage and safety of equipment and also pays dividends if any breakage or damage occurs.

It is usual at the end of a holiday playscheme for a large event to be held which marks the final day of the project. These are often done in conjunction with other playschemes in the area and can take the form of a carnival, fancy dress party or games day. We mention this because we feel that such events ought to be encouraged and that playschemes in which children with disabilities have been participating should be included in such plans. These gatherings bring people together on a large scale to celebrate play, and consequently everyone should be involved.

Once a scheme has finished it is useful for those who have organised it, and the staff who have run it, to sit down and reflect on what went on. What were the strong points and what were the weaknesses? Was staffing adequate? Did the transport operate smoothly? Was the building suitable? Was there enough equipment? Could the project have taken more children? From discussing such areas of concern lessons can be learnt and the programme and planning adapted for the next holiday playscheme. It is at this time that good committees and organisations start planning for the next project. It is no use trying to start planning a summer holiday scheme in June; action has to be taken back in January and February, especially as far as fund-raising, securing premises and arranging transport are concerned. The main message of this chapter is therefore: plan early!

Finally, we need to mention playschemes within mental handicap hospitals. These are discussed in Chapter 8, but we do need to add several campaigning points in this part of the book.

Long-stay hospitals provide a service which the authors of this book would like to see phased out as soon as possible. The 1959 Mental Health Act talked about community care and decanting residents from these large institutions back into the mainstream of community life, but despite numerous government reports and scandals about conditions in such facilities, as instanced by the enquiries into conditions at Ely and Normansfield, there has been no major change of policy. We still have our mental handicap hospitals. The reality is that they will be with us for some time to come, and so it is important that we make life for residents in these institutions as pleasant and profitable as possible. Providing play and recreational facilities is one way of doing this.

It becomes the responsibility of those of us both inside and outside the hospital setting to promote and advise on the creation of play opportunities for residents. Organising holiday, weekend or day playschemes is one of the most immediate and direct ways of doing this.

As with community-based projects, there can be both an indoor and an outdoor element to such projects, but, most importantly, we recommend that full-time staff are appointed to run these schemes. Without such staff it will be extremely difficult to run effective programmes, so money needs to be found from either voluntary or statutory sources to fund these posts. Ideally, appointments should be full-time, but, failing this, part-time posts should be created. Such posts should be seen as an integral part of the services that a hospital has to offer its residents.

Save the Children Fund, along with a number of other organisations, including the Spastics Society, MENCAP, PLAY MATTERS and the National Playing Fields Association, have set up a committee to promote such provision within hospitals, and should be contacted for advice and information.

There is no doubt in our minds that where playschemes in hospitals have been established they have proved to be a great success and have started to meet a huge need for a very deprived section of our population.

Playschemes provide an important and valued service to all children. There are a growing number of schemes being developed for children with disabilities and this needs to be encouraged by both statutory and voluntary services. Our discussion of playschemes is a recognition of their worth and the need for their continued growth in all settings.

11 Charlie Chaplin – a Case History

The Charlie Chaplin Adventure Playground for Handicapped Children in Kennington, South London, is the fifth playground to have been established by the Handicapped Adventure Playground Association (HAPA), and was set up as a joint venture between HAPA and the London Borough of Lambeth – a useful example of the possibility of co-operation between voluntary and statutory bodies.

There had been some discussion between HAPA and Lambeth in the early 1970s, about the possibility of establishing a playground in the borough's Larkhall Park, following the undoubted success of the original Chelsea Playground. This would have been HAPA's second playground. Although these talks produced no immediate result, in 1976 Councillor Bright, Chair of Lambeth's Amenities Committee, invited representatives of HAPA to a meeting to discuss the possibility of establishing a playground on a site adjoining Kennington Park, in the North of the borough.

HAPA expressed interest in this proposal, and stated that they could raise some or all of the capital cost of such a playground, but declared firmly that neither they nor the Inner London Education Authority would be able to meet the running costs. (It is worth noting that revenue funding is often a bigger obstacle to projects such as this than are capital costs – partly because an assurance of revenue funding makes it easier to raise donations towards the capital costs.) It was finally agreed that HAPA would raise half the capital cost and be responsible for administration of the project; Lambeth would provide the other half of the capital and guarantee revenue funding, including the salaries of four playworkers. Lambeth's share of the capital, and initial revenue costs, were met by grants from the Department of the Environment under the Inner City Partnership programme, which recognises the borough's need for additional resources to respond to the problems of one of the most severely deprived inner-city areas in the country.

In March 1980, HAPA, with funding from Lambeth, appointed a Community Development Worker for the project – a move that was to make a major contribution to its success. Gill Goodwillie, the worker in question, was a qualified community worker who had a number of years' experience as a HAPA playworker, having been Senior Playworker at HAPA's Chelsea playground. Gill's brief was to strengthen and co-ordinate the existing Steering Group, which would eventually become a local Management Committee, to liaise between the various bodies involved in developing the playground (HAPA, Lambeth Council's officers and the architects), to establish contact with local statutory and voluntary groups concerned with disability, to work with Special Schools in the catchment area of the playground and to gain local acceptance of the project by liaising with tenants' organisations and community groups.

Gill's personal experience as a HAPA playworker was of particular value. It meant that the design and planning of Charlie Chaplin profited from the practical experience of other HAPA playgrounds, and that the development of the playground was firmly rooted in a realistic understanding of how a successful handicapped adventure playground operates: this was not to be one of those showpiece projects that impress outsiders with facilities that serve everybody's needs but the children's.

Gill was especially aware of the need for the playground to have a satisfactory relationship with its local community, and the role of a voluntary management committee in achieving this. In a development worker's report dated October 1980, she commented that the role of what was then a steering group was 'to shape and guide the initial development of the project in a way which is sensitive to community needs'. The considerable amount of work that Gill put into building up the steering group with this aim in view ensured that Charlie Chaplin's Management Committee would have a stronger local identity than did any of the other HAPA playgrounds. It currently includes parents of children with disabilities, teachers from local special schools, representatives of local voluntary organisations, people with disabilities and other local residents.

Progress was not altogether smooth. A delay in Department of the Environment approval for the Inner City Partnership grants created an uncertainty which hampered HAPA's efforts to raise money from institutional sources such as charitable trusts and large companies. Although the architects HAPA had chosen for the project, Edward Cullinan Partners, had prepared a scheme and outline planning permission had been obtained, Lambeth realised that there was little chance of clearing the site they had earmarked within a reasonable time; they offered an alternative site nearby, within Kennington Park Extension, and this was accepted. (In that this site was part of a public open space, it is questionable whether it would have been approved had Lambeth not first committed itself to the original site.)

Work on site started in 1981, although not without a final crisis. Three days before work was due to start, the architects were informed that the main gas supply for the nearby Brandon Estate ran directly underneath the site, and under a corner of the proposed building – a fact that should have been revealed in the original surveys. Working overtime, they redesigned the entire building over a single weekend, and work on site was able to start as planned. The playground finally opened in September 1982.

The steering group was formally constituted as a management committee (or, more strictly, a playground management *sub*-committee of HAPA) at an Open Meeting in November 1981. This meeting, roughly equivalent to the annual general meeting of an independent body, was a deliberate gesture by the committee to indicate that it saw itself as being accountable to its local community in a way that went beyond its responsibilities to its parent organisation, and to start to encourage local participation in the playground.

Further participation was encouraged by a number of Working Days on the playground, where volunteers helped clear the site and plant shrubs. Various fund-raising ventures helped to publicise the playground's existence: the committee organised a wet-sponge-throwing stall, judo display and face-painting at local events such as the Lambeth Country Show; a tenants' group on the Brandon Estate held a jumble sale which raised £100 for Charlie Chaplin; a local cinema held a benefit screening of cartoon films – which unfortunately coincided with a brilliantly sunny afternoon. But perhaps the most heartening development of all took place at Archbishop Michael Ramsey School, a local comprehensive, where a teacher who was also a member of the playground Management Committee carried out a project on disability with his pupils. Fired with enthusiasm, they undertook a number of fund-raising schemes, such as a session of sponsored doughnut eating, and, on their own initiative, organised and ran an end-of-term disco, to which they invited a number of the children who would be using the playground – an event that proved highly successful.

In January 1982, we short-listed and interviewed applicants for the post of Senior Playworker. This process forced us to think carefully about the kind of workers the playground needed; and in particular, we had to decide whether to attach greater importance to experience in working with children with disabilities or to experience in adventure play. We decided in favour of the latter, and subsequent experience has shown that we made the right decision. While our playworkers have had few problems in adapting to working with children with disabilities, we have had a number of difficulties with other adults, such as teachers accompanying parties of children from special schools, who have shown a tendency to try to direct children's play or intervene to stop activities they thought 'unsuitable'. (Such cases need tactful handling, and it is important that playworkers recognise that part of their job is to educate others in how an adventure playground operates – much more so than on an ordinary adventure playground, where there are likely to be far fewer other adults on the site.)

This appointment was timed to overlap with the final three months of Gill Goodwillie's tenure as Community Development Worker. Our new playworker, Martin Hawes, spent this period in a detailed induction programme, designed by Gill to enable him to understand his new role and help him feel at ease in the new working situation. It involved learning about the management aspects of the job – Martin would be taking over a number of the functions hitherto fulfilled by Gill – acquiring experience of HAPA and of Charlie Chaplin. It also included a number of placements, with other HAPA playgrounds and with local special schools, where Martin had an opportunity to meet future users of the playground in their everyday environment.

We had appointed our other three workers by July, and the playground opened in September. (We had intended to start in August, with a small summer playscheme for the Brixton Contact a Family group, but unforeseen trouble with the drains delayed our opening.) From the very start, it was clear that there was a huge demand for the playground's facilities; we found ourselves fully booked by local special schools and having to turn down some applicants before the playground had even opened.

Looking back, it is possible to see that we made two fairly serious mistakes at this point. Despite the obvious demand, we should not have taken on such a full timetable to start with; it would have made a good deal more sense to take on a few schools at first, and fill our timetable more gradually as we felt we could cope with the additional pressure. (The danger of this approach would have been that the pressure of playground tasks might not have left workers with time for the necessary development work with potential user groups. A possible solution to this dilemma would have been to have extended the Community Development Worker's tenure to cover the playground's first year of operation.)

We should also have appointed all our staff further in advance of the playground's opening date, to give them time to learn to work together as a team, and to prepare thoroughly for the opening of the playground. We had greatly underestimated the amount of work it takes to bring a brand new playground to full working order: planning activities, building structures, ordering equipment and scrounging for materials, not to mention sorting out such minor but essential administrative details as appointing cleaning staff and establishing a workable system for the petty cash. Ideally, we should also have given all our workers something like the induction course Martin went through.

Our failure to appreciate how much had to be done in the early stages, above and beyond working with the children using the playground, meant that our workers had little time for the most basic practical work on site, let alone trying to improve our facilities, develop the service we were offering or extend our links with the local community. After much discussion, our play-workers presented to the management committee a proposal that we should close the playground for a week; this period would be used partly for carrying out work on the playground, but was primarily intended for our staff to visit the schools who used Charlie Chaplin, and discuss with them the idea that we should cut back our timetable, so that most schools would come fortnightly rather than weekly. The committee agreed to this, and we found that the schools' response was remarkably supportive.

It was not merely the timetable change, and the consequent reduction of pressure on our workers, that made this an important step forward. This was the first really major change in playground policy that had been initiated entirely by the playground staff: it therefore marked a significant shift in the relationship between workers and management. The proposal was a radical one, but radical measures were needed (and the committee should perhaps have been aware of this earlier); had the committee failed to respond positively to this suggestion, the effect on playground morale (already low, because of the strain workers were under and the frustration of being unable to extend our work) would have been very damaging.

We also had a number of practical teething problems with the play building. This was perhaps inevitable: it is extremely difficult for any architect or contractor who lacks direct experience of playgrounds to realise quite how heavily they are used, making it necessary to allow for a degree of wear and tear that would not normally be found even in, for example, a school building. Even where, as in the case of Charlie Chaplin, there has been very full consultation, problems will be revealed once the building is in use. But our most serious difficulty of this sort occurred outside, with our pool, which is raised above ground level; we had not realised from the designs that this would mean that it would not be visible from elsewhere on the site - a particularly serious fault in view of the fact that a path runs round the edge of the pool. When a child of limited mobility fell off a tricycle into the pool and was unable to pull herself out, we could have had a very unpleasant accident had it not been for the vigilance of one of our workers, who spotted the trike lying on its side, knew what child had been riding it and realised that she could not simply have left it and walked away. (An anecdote which illustrates the importance of employing trained and experienced playworkers.) The playground was forced to carry out expensive modifications to lower the water level in the pool. We would suggest that any organisation setting up a large project of this sort should include in its initial calculations of capital cost a sum earmarked to be set aside for adaptations and modifications at the end of the first year of operation.

At the time of writing, Charlie Chaplin has been open for eighteen months, and we are coming to feel a little more like an established project. The playground is now used by several hundred children a week. We have continued building local links, and held an Open Day a couple of months after we started up, so that we could show our thanks to various people who had aided us, by inviting them to come and see what they had helped create; this proved to be a highly successful way of consolidating such relationships. We gained quite a lot of local prestige as a result of a Royal Visit by the Princess of Wales, prompted by the fact that a substantial proportion of our capital had come from the Royal Wedding Fund. (But whether such publicity is worth the ill-feeling that can be aroused among people who feel they ought to have been invited is quite another question.) At the end of our first year, we held a second Open Meeting, at which we reported on the year's activities and elected a new Management Committee: it was, to our delight, well attended by parents, teachers and representatives of local groups. Even more successful was a Working Day a few weeks later, when we painted all our structures with the paint that had been donated to us under the Dulux Community Projects Scheme; with a lot of

volunteer help and the playground providing tea and sand-
wiches, everybody had a very jolly time and a tremendous
amount of work got done. But our most successful large event to
date was the Bonfire Night party we held a couple of months
later, which was attended by a couple of hundred adults and
children. Having mounted a lavish firework display, we broke
even with the aid of a small admission charge, a raffle and the
sale of refreshments, and hope that this will become a useful
fund-raising event in future years.

But we still have important problems to solve. We are
unhappy, for example, with the fact that we are currently used
mainly by parties from special schools, who visit the playground
for fairly short periods, once every one or two weeks during termtime. It is difficult for our workers to build relationships with
individual children when they see them so infrequently; and
when they have both the skills and the facilities for elaborate
creative work such as music workshops and photography, it is
frustrating that children are not normally on the playground for
long enough to settle down to such activities. Some of the schools
who use Charlie Chaplin would be happy to bring children for
entire days at a time, and we are currently trying to work out
how we might rearrange our timetable to allow them to do this.

We also want to change the balance of our provision so that
we cater more for individual local children. At present, we are
only open to individuals, as distinct from school parties, on
Saturdays and during the school holidays. Schools can at least
provide alternative activities if they are unable to use Charlie
Chaplin, but many handicapped children are confined to their
homes when not at school. (The parents of one Down's
Syndrome child who uses the playground on Saturdays have
commented that Charlie Chaplin has 'transformed our lives',
now that they can go out shopping on a Saturday leaving Billy
safe and happy on the playground.) As we are only a few
hundred yards from the borough boundary, and are used by
schools and individual children from Southwark, we are
currently negotiating for funding for extra staff, which might
allow us to extend our opening hours.

We know there are many local children with disabilities who

do not use Charlie Chaplin yet; we need to locate those families and let them know about the playground. We should also like to find some way of arranging transport, so that we could go out and fetch children whose parents may find it difficult to get them to us. And we'd like to move into new areas of work, such as with special care children's homes and clubs for handicapped children. And, looking ahead to the question of what happens as children now using the playground grow older, we'd like to follow Chelsea Playground's example, and set up a youth club for mentally handicapped children and young adults.

One difficulty that needs particularly delicate handling is that we often have too many adults around the playground who are not really sympathetic to the philosophy of adventure play. At its most extreme, this produces incidents like the occasion when one of our workers gave a spade to a child who wanted to dig a hole, only to have a teacher take it away a couple of minutes later because she thought the spade was dangerous and digging holes would make the child dirty. More commonly, the presence of a lot of parents sitting around chatting in the kitchen creates an adult atmosphere which children are likely to find restricting; they can no longer feel that the playground belongs to them. This is serious, because it means that children are likely to feel less free to experiment, and therefore get much less benefit from the playground than they should.

There is no single answer to this difficulty; our response needs to consist of a number of different approaches: educating adults about adventure play – at least enough to prevent them from stopping children doing the things for which the playground exists, and preferably to the point where they will positively encourage children and help them to use the playground as fully as possible; encouraging parents to bring their children to the playground and leave them on their own; persuading parents who use the playground to adopt a lower profile and use the area that we have set aside for them out of the kids' way. But all these approaches call for considerable tact and diplomacy if we are to avoid simply alienating these people.

An exciting experiment is currently taking place as the result of a collaboration between Charlie Chaplin and a nearby special school. Aspen House, a school for delicate children, has set up a weekly support group for single parents (of children at the school) who have particular difficulties due to such causes as bereavement, disability, non-attendance at school or illiteracy. While the school social worker and a senior teacher work with these parents at the school, the children attend another group at Charlie Chaplin, run by a teacher, a school care worker and one of our playworkers. This is an experimental scheme, running initially for a fixed period, after which its success will be evaluated, but it looks likely to extend the services offered by both the school and the playground.

The more we accomplish, the more we become aware of further things we should be doing. There is no question of the need for our facilities. And we are just one playground, serving a limited area of South London. In this country alone, there is a real need, not just for the present twenty or so, but for hundreds of handicapped adventure playgrounds. Who will create them?

12 Reference Section

PLAYGROUND CHECKLIST
This is a checklist of basic elements to be considered in the early stages of planning an adventure playground for handicapped children. (For more explicit details see Chapter 3.)

Total size of site (including space for playhut): 1–1½ acres.

Outdoor Site
1　Type of drainage.
2　Presence of trees, bushes, grass.
3　Undulating parts of site.
4　Fencing and main entrance area.
5　Access on to and around site.
6　Areas for play structures.
7　Area for sand and water.
8　Flat area for ball games, use of inflatables, barbecue.
9　Site surveyed for underground obstacles.

Play Building
1　Large play room, containing:
　　a)　Craft area.
　　b)　Space for internal play structures (not essential).
　　c)　'Quiet corner' with easy chairs.
　　d)　Toys and games.
2　Office with telephone.
3　Kitchen.
4　Lavatories with washing facilities.
5　Laundry room.
6　Staff lavatory with lockers.
7　Good storage space: shelving and store rooms.
8　Flooring.

9 Heating system.
10 Access.
11 Lighting: Overall lightness and amount of natural light.

EXISTING ADVENTURE PLAYGROUNDS FOR HANDICAPPED CHILDREN

Attlee Adventure Playground, Flower and Dean Street (off Commercial Street), London E1. 01-247 1281

Basildon and District Handicapped Adventure Playground, c/o 4, Laburnum Avenue, Wickford, Essex, SS12 0DD. (037) 44 3132

Beckley Adventure Playground, Beckley Family Unit, Scott Hospital, Beacon Park Road, Plymouth, South Devon. (0752) 51437

Calderstones Park Adventure Playground, Harthill Road, Calderstones Park, Liverpool 18. (051) 725 2240

Charlie Chaplin Adventure Playground (HAPA), Bolton Crescent, Kennington, London SE5 1AA. 01-735 1819

Chelsea Adventure Playground (HAPA), Royal Hospital South Ground, Royal Hospital Road, London SW3. 01-730 4093

Ealing Log Cabin Playground, 259 Northfield Avenue, Ealing, London W5. 01-840 3400

East London Handicapped Adventure Playground, 119 Roding Lane North, Woodford Bridge, Essex. 01-550 2636

Fulham Palace Adventure Playground (HAPA), Fulham Palace, Bishops Avenue, Fulham, London SW6. 01-731 2753

Gloucester Special Adventure Playground, Seven Springs, Cheltenham, Gloucestershire, GL53 9WG. (024) 287 438

Guildford Adventure Playground, Guildford Adventurers Association, Bramlyn House, Linersh Wood Close, Bramley, Surrey. (0483) 893563

Hayward Adventure Playground (HAPA), Market Road Gardens, Market Road, Islington, London N1. 01-607 0033

Jonathan Page Adventure Playground, Manor House Hospital, Stocklake, Aylesbury, Buckinghamshire. (0296) 748 711 Ext. 5132

Lady Allen Adventure Playground (HAPA), Chivalry Road,

Wandsworth Common, London SW11. 01-228 0278

Park View Adventure Playground, Park View, Huyton, Merseyside. (051) 4899366

St Lawrence's Hospital Playground, St Lawrence's Hospital, Caterham, Surrey. (0883) 46411

Scottish Adventure Playground Association for Handicapped Children, Netherlee Road, Glasgow, G44. (041) 633 1493

Thames Valley Adventure Playground Association, Bath Road, Taplow, Near Maidenhead, Berkshire. (0628) 2859

Society for Disabled Children's Playgrounds, Haifa, PO Box 289, Israel.

The June Peckover Adventure Playground for Handicapped Children, PO Box 90, Rydalmere, NSW 2116, Australia.

Kasugai City Adventure Playground for Handicapped Children, c/o Institute for Developmental Research, Aichi Prefectural Colony, Kamiya-Cho, Kasugai, Aichi 480-03, Japan.

PUBLICATIONS

Adventure Playgrounds for Handicapped Children (Handicapped Adventure Playground Association). Booklet describing HAPA's work, and presenting practical advice on setting up and running playgrounds, based on HAPA's experience. Available from HAPA.

All Children Play. Information pack on play in multi-racial Britain, produced by Fair Play for Children. Available from PLAY BOARD.

Lady Allen of Hurtwood: *Planning for Play* (Thames and Hudson, 1975). Major work on design aspects of play provision, aimed primarily at town-planners and architects, by one of the pioneers of adventure play, herself a landscape architect.

Marjory Allen and Mary Nicholson: *Memoirs of an Uneducated Lady: Lady Allen of Hurtwood.* (Thames and Hudson, 1975). Lady Allen's autobiography.

Sean Andrews and Ciaran O'Connor: *Space for Play* (Comhchairideas, Dublin, 1980).

Ark. Magazine produced by PLAY MATTERS linking toy libraries. Includes information about toys that will be included in the next Good Toy Guide.

Arnold Arnold: *Your Child's Play* (Pan, 1975).

Arvid Bengtsson: *Adventure Playgrounds* (Crosby Lockwood, 1972).

Arvid Bengtsson: *The Child's Right to Play* (International Play Association, 1974).

Joe Benjamin: *Grounds for Play* (Bedford Square Press of the National Council for Social Service, 1974). Major study of the development of the adventure play movement in Britain.

Leila Berg: *Look at Kids* (Penguin, 1972).

Hilary Blume: *Fund-raising – A Comprehensive Handbook* (Routledge and Kegan Paul, 1977).

Agatha Hilliam Bowley and Leslie Gardner: *The Handicapped Child* (Churchill Livingstone, 1972). Background.

Kenneth Boyes, Sandra Franklin (Eds): *Design for the Handicapped* (George Godwin Ltd, 1971). Specialist American architectural publication, with papers on: mentally retarded; mentally ill; the maladjusted; the blind; the deaf; those with learning disabilities; the gifted child.

Jerome S. Bruner, A. Jolly and K. Sylva: *Play: Its Role in Development and Evolution* (Penguin, 1976). Comprehensive examination of all aspects of play.

Bernice Wells Carlson and D. R. Ginglend: *Play Activities for the Retarded Child* (Baillière Tindall, 1961). Early book on play and disability.

Janet Carr: *Helping Your Handicapped Child: A Step by Step Guide* (Penguin, 1980).

Don Caston: *Easy to Make Toys for Your Handicapped Child* (Souvenir Press, 1983). Instructions for making 60 toys for handicapped children.

Charities Digest (published annually by Family Welfare Association, 501–5 Kingsland Road, Dalston, London E8 4AU, Macdonald and Evans Ltd). A hefty reference book – an important tool if you're setting about raising large amounts of funding. Should be in your local reference library.

Steve Clarke: *Working on a Committee* (from Community Projects Foundation, Publications Dept, Central Resource Unit, 7 Leonard Street, London EC2 4AQ).

The Community Involvement Resource Pack (Young Volunteers Resources Unit, National Youth Bureau, 16–23 Albion Street, Leicester). Information and advice on how projects can increase community involvement.

Brenda Crowe: *Play is a Feeling* (George Allen and Unwin, 1983). Although we have not read this book, it has been strongly recommended to us by several people who are experienced in the field of play.

Ann Darnborough and Derek Kinrade: *Fund-raising and Grant-aid: A practical and legal guide for charities and voluntary organisations* (Woodhead-Faulkner, Cambridge, 1980.) A good starting-point for the process of raising finances for a playground project.

Directory of Grant-Making Trusts (Charities Aid Foundation). Another useful fund-raising tool, which should be next to the *Charities Digest* on the library shelf.

Erica Eden: *Enjoy Being an Editor* (PPA, 1983). Booklet of practical hints and tips on producing a newsletter.

Warren Feek: *Talk about Management.* A series of booklets about managing community-based agencies with a good collection of practical checklists. Available from the Sales Department, National Youth Bureau, 16–23 Albion Street, Leicester.

Barbara Furneaux: *The Special Child* (Penguin, 1981). Background.

Tony Gibson: *People Power: Community and Work Groups in Action* (Penguin, 1979). Describes the experiences of a large number of self-help action groups. Its 140-page 'Fact Bank' is an invaluable source of related practical information.

The Good Toy Guide (Annually, from PLAY MATTERS/ A. & C. Black Publishers Ltd). Includes a section of 'Toys for people with special needs'.

The Great Play Times Games Kit (NPFA, 1983). 250 cards of (mainly non-competitive) games for playschemes and playgrounds, 'specially designed for informal situations'.

Guide to Effective Meetings (The Industrial Society, Peter Runge

House, 3 Carlton House Terrace, London SW1Y 5DG. 01–839 4300). Booklet about how to conduct meetings.

Glorya Hale (Ed): *The New Source Book for the Disabled* (William Heinemann, 1983).

Susan Harvey and Ann Hales-Tooke (Eds): *Play in Hospital* (Faber and Faber, 1972). Mainly concerned with work on the ward, but does contain a section on children with special problems.

David Harwood: *The Extension Activities Handbook – A Guide to Scouting with the Handicapped* (Scout Association, 1972). Includes helpful information on activities like camping, and a useful introductory run-down of the nature of various disabilities.

Peter Henderson: *Disability in Childhood and Youth* (OUP, 1974).

Joan Hill: *Play for the Handicapped Child* (Wiltshire County Council Education Department, 1982. Available from County Hall, Trowbridge, Wiltshire). Booklet.

How to make a playscheme (booklet, available from Manchester Council for Voluntary Services, The Gaddum Centre, 274 Deansgate, Manchester, M3 4FT.)

How to Organise a Holiday Playscheme (NPFA, 1983). A pack designed for parents and others wanting to organise a holiday playscheme from scratch. Includes details on management and emergency procedures, and a section on suggested activities.

Bob Hughes: *Notes for Adventure Playworkers* (Children and Youth Action Group, 1975).

Insurance for Children's Play (NPFA, 1983). Covers all the legal and financial aspects of an important subject for playground or playscheme managements.

Jay Report: See *Mental Handicap Nursing and Care.*

Dorothy M. Jeffree, Roy McConkey and Simon Hewson: *Let Me Play* (Souvenir Press, 1977).

Dorothy M. Jeffree and Margaret Skeffington: *Let Me Read* (Souvenir Press, 1980).

Chris Kiernan, Rita Jordan, Chris Saunders: *Starting Off: Establishing Play and Communication in the Handicapped Child* (Souvenir Press, 1978).

Frank King: *Structures for Adventure Playgrounds* (NPFA, 1984).

We expect this 'introduction to structure building for community groups and playworkers', still in the press at the time of writing, to be a major contribution to the field. Topics covered range 'from design to construction, from joints to surfacing'.

Jack Lambert and Jenny Pearson: *Adventure Play* (Jonathan Cape, 1974; Penguin 1974). Useful introduction to the adventure play approach via a seasoned playleader's account of his experiences.

Roma Lear: *Play Helps: Toys and Activities for Handicapped Children* (Heinemann Medical, 1977). Useful handbook on play activities, dealing mainly with indoor play in such contexts as playgroups and toy libraries.

A. J. Leicester: *Integrating Disabled Children in Play: A Guide to Organising an Integrated Playscheme or Junior Youth Club.* Valuable primer for integrated schemes, available from Sheffield Children's Integrated Play Association (SKIP). Free to Sheffield organisations.

Sophie Levitt: *A study of the gross motor skills of cerebral palsied children in an adventure playground for handicapped children.* Study based on work done at Chelsea playground. Available for reference from HAPA.

Pete Limbrick (Ed): *One to One – An Experiment with Community Participation in Long-stay Hospitals* (Inter-Action Inprint, 1976. Available from 15 Wilkin Street, London NW5).

Ivonny Lindquist: *Therapy through Play* (Arlington Books, 1977).

Michael Locke: *How to Run Committees and Meetings: a guide book to practical politics* (Macmillan, 1980). Detailed and accessible guide to committee activities and procedures.

Roy McConkey and Dorothy M. Jeffree: *Let's Make Toys* (Souvenir Press, 1981).

Denis MacShane: *Using the Media: How to Deal with the Press, Television and Radio* (Pluto Press, 1979). An invaluable source of practical information.

Mental Handicap Nursing and Care (Jay Report), (HMSO, 1979).

Susanna Millar: *The Psychology of Play* (Penguin 1971).

Ivan Nellist: *Planning Buildings for Handicapped Children* (Crosby,

Lockwood and Sons, 1970). Mainly concerned with day centres, special schools, etc., but useful on practical design details, with a lot of simple diagrams.

John and Elizabeth Newson et al.: *Toys and Playthings: in development and remediation* (Penguin, 1978). Includes chapter on play and disability.

Organising a Playscheme – a step by step guide to organising a summer playscheme in Glasgow. Booklet published by Strathclyde Regional Council.

Maureen Oswin: *Children Living in Long-stay Hospitals* (Spastics International Medical Publications, London/Heinemann Medical, 1978).

Maureen Oswin: *The Empty Hours: Weekend Life of Handicapped Children in Institutions* (Allen Lane, 1971).

PHAB Startakit. A resource pack for anyone wanting to start a PHAB (Physically Handicapped/Able Bodied) Club. Available from National PHAB (see Organisations).

Play Aids for the Handicapped Child. From Handicapped Persons Research Unit, Newcastle on Tyne Polytechnic, 1 Coach Lane, Coach Lane Campus, Newcastle on Tyne.

Playeducation '82 – The transcript. Transcript of Playeducation's first conference. Available from Playeducation.

Play Mounds (NPFA Technical Department). Covers technical details of how to construct mounds, and includes information on sand and sand pits.

Play and Playwork: Development and Definitions. Transcript of Playeducation's 1983 conference.

Playschemes – A practical handbook (Fair Play for Scotland). Extremely useful pamphlet on how to organise playschemes.

Play Times. Now-defunct magazine published by the NPFA. Back copies of this magazine provide an excellent source of play ideas and information about play.

Play, Toys and Toy Libraries in Mental Handicap Hospitals (Toy Libraries Association).

PLAYTRAC Report (Save the Children Fund, 1983). SCF's report on an important and innovative experimental project, where a travelling resource and advice centre on play and leisure activities was taken around long-stay hospitals for mentally handicapped people, concentrating particularly on training the ward staff who worked with the most profoundly handicapped residents of all ages.

Ann Purser: *You and Your Handicapped Child* (Penguin, 1981).

Running a Summer Adventure Playground (NPFA, 1976). Introduction to the practical aspects of a holiday playscheme based on the adventure playground concept.

Joanna Ryan and Frank Thomas: *The Politics of Mental Handicap* (Penguin, 1980).

Scout Association pamphlets cover a number of areas relevant to playground work, such as structures, knots and splices, games. (Address under Organisations.) See also: *The Extension Activities Handbook*.

H. Shier: *An Introduction to Adventure Playgrounds* (NPFA, 1984).

Robin Simons: *Recyclopaedia* (Puffin, 1979). A cheap and handy book, aimed primarily at kids, with lots of useful ideas for things to make out of waste/cheap materials.

Mark Smith: *Organise!: A guide to practical politics for youth and community groups* (National Association of Youth Clubs Political Education Project, 1981). A guide to organising campaigns. Easy to read and understand, with plenty of drawings and cartoons.

Statutes and Constitutions (NPFA). Includes Government Acts under which assistance can be given to children's play, Model Trust Deed and examples of constitutions.

Judith Stone and Felicity Taylor: *A Handbook for Parents with a Handicapped Child* (Arrow Books, 1977).

Allan T. Sutherland: *Disabled We Stand* (Souvenir Press, 1981).

Towards a Safer Adventure Playground (NPFA, 2nd edn, 1984). We can not over-emphasise that this code of practice is essential reading for all playworkers and management committee members.

Chris Treweek and Jonathan Zeitlya: *The Alternative Printing Handbook* (Penguin, 1983).

Sylvia Valentine: *A Fund of Ideas* (PPA, 1983). Booklet of ideas on local fund-raising schemes.

Voluntary but not Amateur (London Voluntary Service Council, 68 Charlton Street, London, NW1 1JR). Guide to the law for voluntary organisations and community groups.

Voluntary Organisations Directory (MacDonald and Evans). Lists over 600 national organisations, with a brief summary of their aims and objectives.

Colin Ward: *The Child in the City* (Architectural Press, 1978).

Chris Wardle: *City Farming and Community Gardening, Book 1* (Inter-Action Inprint, 1983. Available from: 15 Wilkin Street, London NW5). Describes how to get a project started. Book 2, on how to run a city farm, is due out in 1984.

Barbara F. Weller: *Helping Sick Children Play* (Baillière Tindall, 1980). Includes a useful chapter on ideas suitable for play activities.

Who are you staring at? (Community Service Volunteers). Information pack concerning disability awareness, for use with volunteers and other groups of workers.

D. W. Winnicott: *Playing and Reality* (Penguin, 1974).

Paul Wolff: *The Adventure Playground as a Therapeutic Environment* 1980. A thesis based on research done at Chelsea playground. For details contact Professor Wolff at California Polytechnic State University, San Luis Obispo, Cal. 93407.

ORGANISATIONS

This list does not include local groups, with the exception of a few particular cases which we have mentioned in the text or feel may have a wider interest to readers. For details of local groups and organisations in the field of play in your area, contact your local PLAY BOARD Play Development Officer. Nor have we tried to cover the vast range of charities and other organisations dealing with specific disabilities, or particular aspects of disability, unless they are especially active in the field of play or have been mentioned in the text.

ACTIVE (For address, see PLAY MATTERS). Organisation within PLAY MATTERS (The National Toy Libraries Association) which promotes play and leisure activities, communication and other aids for disabled people, and encourages the formation of ACTIVE groups all over the British Isles. It also publishes a series of worksheets for making specially designed and adapted toys for people with special needs.

British Red Cross Society, 9 Grosvenor Crescent, London SW1. 01-235 5454.

Castle Priory College, Thames Street, Wallingford, Oxon, OX10 0HE. (0491) 37551.

Charity Commission, 14 Ryder Street, London, SW1Y 6AH. 01-214 6000. Statutory body governing registered charities. Contact them for details of how to register as a charity.

Children's Scrap Project, 137 Homerton High Street, London E9. 01-985 6290. (See also: Federation of Resource Centres).

City Farm Advisory Service, 15 Wilkin Street, London, NW5 3NX. 01-267 9421. Contact for the address of your nearest city farm, or information about the city farm movement.

Cleveland Playschemes Association, c/o Margaret Hoggarth, Cleveland Council for Voluntary Service, Princes House, 47 Princes Road, Middlesbrough, Cleveland. (0642) 240651.

Community Service Volunteers, 237 Pentonville Road, London N1. 01-278 6601. National organisation concerned with placing volunteers; existing playgrounds have benefited from their work. They produce an information pack, *Who are you staring at?*, concerning disability awareness.

Contact a Family, 16 Strutton Ground, London SW1. 01-222 2695. Organisation that sets up and advises self-help groups for families containing children with disabilities.

Diploma in Playleadership Course, Thurrock Technical College, Woodview, Grays, Essex. (0375) 71621.

Disabled Living Foundation, 346 Kensington High Street, London W14. 01-602 2491. Useful source of details of equipment and aids.

Fair Play for Children Association, 137 Homerton High Street, London, E9. This organisation has grown out of the closure of the Fair Play for Children Charitable Trust, whose co-ordinating role has been taken over by PLAY BOARD. The

Association has no full-time staff, and is formulating its aims and objectives at the time of writing.

Fair Play for Children in Scotland, 39 Hope Street, Glasgow, G2 6AE, Scotland. (041) 204 2300. Co-ordinating body for play in Scotland. Gives advice and information on a variety of play activities and organisations.

Federation of Resource Centres, Midlands Resource Centre, Ward End Park, Washwood Heath Road, Birmingham 8. (021) 328 5557. Contact for list of existing Scrap projects.

Glasgow Playschemes Association, c/o Jeely Piece Club, Castlemilk, Glasgow, G45. (041) 634 73050.

Mike Halward (Children's Play Consultant), 35 Aylesbury Street, Wolverton, Milton Keynes. (0908) 314536. Offers advice on safety and design of children's playground areas.

Handicapped Adventure Playground Association (HAPA), Fulham Palace, Bishops Avenue, London, SW6 6EA. 01-736 4443. The organisation with the greatest experience in the field of adventure play with handicapped children, HAPA currently runs five London playgrounds, but has, for financial reasons, cut back drastically on its national field work and information services to other playgrounds. HAPA produce the *HAPA Journal* three times a year.

International Organisation for the Child's Right to Play (formerly the International Play Association). For information, contact the Secretary: Nancy Ovens, 3 Denham Green Avenue, Edinburgh, EH5 3NY.

International Voluntary Service (IVS), 53 Regent Road, Leicester. (0533) 541862.

Joint National Committee for Training for Playleadership, c/o Christine Taylor, Diploma Course in Playleadership, Thurrock Technical College, Woodview, Grays, Essex. (0375) 71621 Ext. 268. An organisation concerned with the standards and organisation of training for playworkers nationally.

Kith and Kids, c/o Thomas Coram Foundation, 40 Brunswick Square, London, WC1N 1AZ. 01-278 3459.

London Adventure Playground Association (LAPA), 28 Underwood Road, London, E1 5AW. 01-377 0314.

MENCAP (Royal Society for Mentally Handicapped Children and Adults), 123 Golden Lane, London, EC1Y 0RT. 01-253 9433. National organisation involved in field of mental handicap. Contact central office for information on local MENCAP groups and their wide range of publications.

Merseyside Play Action Council, 124 Duke Street, Liverpool 1. (051) 708 0468.

Midlands Play Train, c/o NPFA Resource Centre, Ward End Park, Washwood Heath Road, Birmingham 8. (021) 328 5557. Provides a mobile training workshop and advice service in the Midlands area – an idea that could be usefully followed elsewhere.

National Association for the Welfare of Children in Hospital, 7 Exton Street, London, SE1 8UE. 01-261 1738. Provides support for children confined to hospital, and their families.

National Association of Hospital Play Staff, c/o Thomas Coram Children's Centre, 40 Brunswick Square, London, WC1.

National Council for Voluntary Organisations, 26 Bedford Square, London, WC1. 01-636 4066. Co-ordinating body for voluntary organisations. They issue regular newsletters and run an information service.

National Out of School Alliance, Oxford House, Derbyshire Street, off Bethnal Green Road, London E2 6HG. 01-739 4787. Grouping of organisations concerned with recreational activities outside school hours, and campaigning for more and better use of school premises. They produce an information pack, *Starting from Scratch*, on starting out-of-school activities.

National Playbus Association, St Thomas's Church, St Thomas's Street, Bristol, BS1. (0272) 25951. Produce a pack, *Working on Wheels*, which gives a very comprehensive guide to playbus work – how to make them and what activities to do.

National Playing Fields Association (NPFA), 25 Ovington Square, London, SW3 1LQ. 01-584 6445. Formerly a major organisation in the field of play, the NPFA have curtailed their activities severely with the establishment of PLAY BOARD, but still have a useful list of publications available and a technical department which can offer advice on structural and design aspects of playgrounds. The NPFA also operate a grants and loan scheme to play projects. Their Midlands Resource Centre is still in operation.

National Standing Conference. Grouping of workers on handicapped adventure playgrounds and others concerned with handicapped adventure play, who run regular weekend workshops. For details, contact your nearest handicapped adventure playground.

New Games, 11 Plato Road, London, SW2 5UP. Organisation which encourages non-competitive games.

Northern Ireland Play Development Association, Play Resource Warehouse, 88 Tomb Street, Belfast BT1. (0232) 230738.

One to One, 123–25 Gloucester Place, London, W1H 3PJ. 01–486 0074/5. Organisation which works in long-stay hospitals, pairing volunteers with individual residents.

PHAB. National PHAB, 42 Devonshire Street, London, W1N 1LN. 01–637 7475. For information about your nearest PHAB (Physically Handicapped/Able Bodied) Club. More generally, a source of information on integrated youth clubs and playschemes.

PLAY BOARD, Britannia House, 50 Great Charles Street, Queensway, Birmingham, B3 2LP. (021) 233 3399. This newly-established national organisation, which is to take over many of the roles previously performed by such organisations as the NPFA and Fair Play for Children, is at the time of writing still at the planning and development stage. It is therefore difficult to state with any precision how it will operate in detail.

PLAY BOARD aims to encourage and promote the development of children through play and recreation. Its stated objectives are: to promote facilities for play, recreation and other leisure-time opportunities for children; to carry out, encourage, commission and publish research into children's play and recreation; to provide an educational, advisory, information and promotional service for children's play and recreation; to provide a co-ordinating and development role with voluntary organisations concerned with children's play and recreation.

The organisation will appoint a number of Regional Play

Development Officers throughout England; the organisation's brief does not at present cover the rest of the British Isles. It will also appoint a member of staff with specific responsibility for Special Needs. It will produce regular publications, and a range of other materials, including audio-visual materials.

This is potentially a major development in play provision. Readers are encouraged to contact PLAY BOARD directly for more detailed information than is available to the present authors at the time of writing.

PLAYEDUCATION, 97 Dale Street, Lancaster. (0524) 34439. Organise conferences and produce useful publications on play, including in particular the transcripts of their annual conferences. (See also Publications).

Play in Hospital Liaison Committee, c/o Pre-school Playgroups Association, Save the Children Fund, the National Association for the Welfare of Children in Hospital and the British Association of Early Childhood Education. Grouping of organisations concerned with play in all hospital settings.

PLAY MATTERS/National Toy Libraries Association, Seabrook House, Potters Bar, Herts EN6 2HL. 01-774 4571. For the address of your nearest Toy Library, and information on how to start one. Their publications include *Ark* and the annual *Good Toy Guide*.

Play Resource Unit, Moray House College of Education, Holyrood Road, Edinburgh, EH8 8AQ, Scotland. (031) 556 8455.

Pre-School Playgroups Association (PPA), Alford House, Aveline Street, London SE11. 01-582 8871. Organisation co-ordinating pre-school play provision for the under-fives. Their Opportunity Groups section deals with pre-school play for children with disabilities and integrated pre-school playgroups.

Quaker Work Camps, Friends House, Euston Road, London NW1 2BJ. 01-387 3601.

RADAR, 25 Mortimer Street, London W1. 01-637 5400.

Riding for the Disabled Association, Avenue Road, Kenilworth, Warwickshire, CV8 2LR. (0203) 56107.

St John Ambulance, 1 Grosvenor Crescent, London SW1. 01-235 5231. For first aid courses.

Save the Children Fund, Mary Datchelor House, Camberwell Grove, London, SE5 8RD. 01–703 5400. This international organisation's work includes play provision in long-stay hospitals and some community-based playschemes.

Scout Association, Baden Powell House, 65 Queen's Gate, London SW7. Publications can provide useful information about such subjects as camping and knots. Their special sections, Extension Scouting and Extension Guiding, cater specifically for children with disabilities and could be worth contacting if planning a camping weekend, for example.

Sheffield Children's Integrated Play Association (SKIP), 124 Devonshire Street, Sheffield, S3 7SF. (0742) 26609. Very active local organisation: see Chapter 9 for further details.

The Spastics Society, 12 Park Crescent, London, W1N 4EQ. 01–636 5020.

Toy Libraries Association. Renamed: see PLAY MATTERS.

Voluntary Council for Handicapped Children, 8 Wakley Street, London, EC1V 7QE. 01–278 9441.

Voluntary Sector Combine 1983, c/o TUCRIC, Market Buildings, Vicar Lane, Leeds 1. (0532) 439633. Grouping of trades unions which issues guidelines on conditions of service in the voluntary sector.

The Volunteer Centre, 29 Lower King's Road, Berkhampstead, Herts, HP4 2AB. (044) 27 73311. An organisation which provides information, advice and publications on working with volunteers.

AUDIO-VISUAL MATERIALS

Towards a Safer Playground (Tape/slide). A valuable and entertaining introduction to playground health and safety procedures. We strongly recommend this as a tool for training sessions with playground management or staff. Available from LAPA for sale or hire.

Summerville Road (Videotape). A day in the life of a LAPA playground. Available from LAPA.

An Adventure Playground for the Handicapped (16mm film. Optical sound). Available from CFL vision, Charlfont Grove,

Gerrard's Cross, Bucks. SL9 8TN. (02407) 4433. Film Ref. No. U.K.3099. Central Office of Information Film made in the early days of the original Chelsea Playground. Also available on videotape from HAPA.

HAPA's information service possesses a substantial collection of slides and photographs taken on their playgrounds.

Some local projects have videotapes or slides showing their work; it might be worth checking this out with local playgrounds.

Local Health Education Units may have relevant films or videotapes, and will certainly be able to help with ordering material from distributors. They will also loan relevant equipment, such as projectors and screens.

PLAY BOARD will be producing a range of audio-visual materials about play.

SOURCES OF EQUIPMENT

All the following suppliers and manufacturers of equipment have been found to be reliable by such organisations as ACTIVE and HAPA. Most of them supply equipment by mail order, and have catalogues available on request. If you have more detailed queries about toys and play equipment, contact PLAY MATTERS for advice.

Aremco, Grove House, Lenham, Kent ME17 2PX. (0622) 858502. Hasi tricycles in three sizes. Enormous range of special adaptations.

E. J. Arnold & Sons Ltd/ESA, Parkside Lane, Dewsbury Road, Leeds, LS11 5TD. (0532) 772112. Educational games and toys that can be used by handicapped children, including Saddle Seat Engines (two sizes), Transporter Trolley (hand propelled), Mini and Maxi Trikes (see Searles Tuffa).

Bowley and Coleman Trucks Ltd, Lye Trading Estate, 137/141 Old Bedford Road, Luton, Beds. Play trolleys and trucks – very sturdy, highly recommended equipment.

British Toy and Hobby Manufacturers Association, 80 Camberwell Road, London SE5 OE6. 01-701 7271. Umbrella body.

Byrd's, Ashton under Hill, Evesham, Worcester. (0386) 881297. Buggy car – two hand levers control direction, speed and braking. Optional backrest.

Canning Leisure Co. Ltd, Sandy Lane Industrial Estate, Worksop C80. Safety surfaces.

Chailey Rehabilitation Engineering Unit, Chailey Heritage, Lewes, East Sussex, BN8 4EF. (082 572) 2112. Footplate, strap and optional side steel for adapting pedals yourself.

Clatterway Toys, 31 Watton Road, Colney, Norwich, Norfolk. (0603) 810471. Adapted battery-operated toys: range of switches also available.

Community Playthings, Robertsbridge, East Sussex, TN32 5DR. (0580) 880626. Wide range of play equipment, toys and seating.

En Tout Cas, 690 Merton Road, Thurmaston, Leicester LE4 8EP. (0533) 696181. Surfaces and wide range of outdoor sports equipment.

Four to Eight Ltd, PO Box 38, Northgates, Leicester, LE1 9BU. (0533) 50405. Front-wheel cranked heavy tricycles with trailers. Very similar to Searles Tuffa.

James Galt and Co Ltd, Brookfield Road, Cheadle, Cheshire SK8 2PN. (061) 428 8511. Toys, play equipment, educational supplies.

ABC Hansen Co., PO Box 3054, 1508 Copenhagen, Denmark. Danish go-kart.

R. C. Hayes (Leicester) Ltd, 12a Wood Street, Earl Shilton, Leicestershire LE9 7ND. (0455) 46027. Jay Bike, Big T Trike, Tow Trike. Lots of individual adaptations.

Hestair Hope Ltd, St Philip's Drive, Royton, Oldham, OL2 6AG. (061) 652 1411. Soft play environment.

Joncare (Meadjess), Radley Road Industrial Estate, Abingdon, Oxon. (0235) 28120. Jonsport trolley, Flying Dutchman trike.

Indicycle, 104 Greencastle Road, Kilkeel, Co. Down, BT34 4AX. (06937) 63235. Hand propelled, using levers in rowing motion.

Leeds and District ACTIVE Toy Project, 3 Roxholme Terrace, Leeds, LS7 4JH. (0532) 622339. Small trike modified to hand propulsion, fore and aft section. Also supplies and adapts toys.

Meyra Rehab UK, Millshaw Park Avenue, Leeds, LS11 0LR. (0532) 776060. Playmobiles – many methods of hand propulsion, excellent support seats.

Newton Aids, *see* Spastics Society (Birmingham). Wheelchairs and special supplies for the handicapped.

NOMEQ, 23–25 Thornhill Road, North Moon Moat, Redditch, B98 9NL. (0527) 63622. Corner seats, rehabilitation equipment, wedges.

Rupert Oliver Designs Ltd, 505 London Road, Croydon, Surrey, CR4 6AR. Soft play/environmental furnishings.

Opal, PO Box 47, Waltham Cross, Herts, EN8 0BS. (0992) 135697. Skatebike – pedalled bike steered by leaning.

W. R. Pashley Ltd, Mason's Road, Stratford-upon-Avon, CV37 9NL. (0789) 292263. Chain driven tricycles from about 4 years to adult.

Photomec (London) Ltd, Valley Road Industrial Estate, St Albans, Herts, AL3 6NU. (0727) 50711. Bitri Converter – turns bike into trike. Optional back support.

Playfactor, Frank Triggs, The Poplars, Gwerning-Brenin, Oswestry, Shropshire. Playfactor design and construct specialised play equipment and aids for handicapped children.

Preston, Camp Therapy, Northgate House, Staple Gardens, Winchester, Hants, SO23 8ST. (0962) 55248. Bikes and trikes, including chain-driven with adaptations.

Prindus, c/o Home Office, Tolworth Tower, Surbiton, Surrey, KT6 7DS. 01–399 5191 Ext. 745. Hobcart – fore and aft rowing hand propelled go-kart, with adult push handle.

Rifton Equipment for the Handicapped, (address/phone as Community Playthings). Scooterboards, hand trolleys. Tricycles, foot and hand propelled.

Searles Tuffa Toys, 34 Telville Road, Worthing, Sussex. (0903) 201017. Heavy-duty Danish trikes, scooters and play equipment in various sizes including adult. Puky bikes, trikes, scooters and go-karts. Highly recommended.

SMP (Landscape) Ltd, Horton Road, Datchet, Berks, SL3 9ES. (0753) 40555. Outdoor play equipment, landscape furniture.

Southwest Designs, Saddlers, Funtington, Chichester, Sussex. Mobile corner seats.

Spastics Society (Birmingham), Meadway Works, Garretts Green Lane, Birmingham, West Midlands, B33 0SQ. (021) 783 6081.

Syddal Engineering, Palatine Street, Denton, Manchester, M34 3QH. (061) 336 4205. Trendsetter Trike – hand-propelled, upholstered seat and backrest.

Target Training Workshop Co., The Albany Works, Gun-makers Lane, London E3 5TT. 01–981 0865. Electric power go-karts and maintenance.

Toy Aids Project, Lodbourne Farmhouse, Lodbourne Green, Gillingham, Dorset SP8 4EH. (074) 76 2256. Range of specially adapted toys for use with severely handicapped children.

Toys for the Handicapped, 76 Barracks Road, Sandilane Industrial Estate, Stourport, Worcs, DY13 9QB. (02993) 78820. Wide range of toys for children with disabilities.

Theramed, PO Box 57, Camberley, Surrey. (0276) 27060. Rowcar – fore and aft hand-propelled go-kart. Flying Dutch-man hand-operated tricycle.

Three Jays Co. Ltd, 9 The Precinct, High Road, Broxbourne, Herts. Waterproof clothing, wet-suits, anoraks. HAPA wet-suits are made with waterproof fabric from this firm, using Simplicity pattern 7162 (clown's suit).

Tri Aid Manufacturing Ltd, 63 James Watt Place, College Milton North, East Kilbride, Lanarkshire G74 5HG. (035 52) 33133. Thistle hand-cranked tricycles in three sizes.

Western Medical Ltd, 26 New Cavendish Street, London, W1M 7LH. 01–935 7209/7210/8145. Hasi range – see Aremco.

WRK Developments, Ashfield House, School Road, Fen End, Terrington St John, Wisbech, Cambs. (0945) 880014. Supa Pedalong, Supa Byke (three sizes), Supa Rolling Boat, Supa Flying Dutchman. Lots of individual adaptations.

Index